A History of Some of London's Most Famous Landmarks

By Charles River Editors

A 1900 stereocard of Tower Bridge

About Charles River Editors

Charles River Editors is a boutique digital publishing company, specializing in bringing history back to life with educational and engaging books on a wide range of topics. Keep up to date with our new and free offerings with this 5 second sign up on our weekly mailing list, and visit Our Kindle Author Page to see other recently published Kindle titles.

We make these books for you and always want to know our readers' opinions, so we encourage you to leave reviews and look forward to publishing new and exciting titles each week.

Introduction

Westminster Abbey

"It is eerie being all but alone in Westminster Abbey. Without the tourists, there are only the dead, many of them kings and queens. They speak powerfully and put my thoughts into vivid perspective." – A.N. Wilson

It almost goes without saying that Westminster Abbey is one of the foremost sites in Europe when it comes to being steeped in history. Dating back to the reign of William the Conqueror and the Norman conquest, Westminster Abbey has traditionally been the site of royal coronations, royal weddings, and royal burials, and anyone who enters can instantly feel that they are walking in the footsteps of some of the most influential figures in history, from Henry III to Queen Elizabeth I.

Of course, Westminster Abbey is also far more than a place for royalty. As the English became to more intimately associate the site with their history and culture, luminaries from all walks of life have also been interred there, from Charles Darwin and Isaac Newton to Rudyard Kipling and Charles Dickens. Along with effigies, plaques, and various other monuments, walking through Westminster Abbey offers its own sort of crash course on England over the centuries.

While Westminster Abbey has been an important site for nearly 1,000 years, it is perhaps unsurprising that it has had a volatile history, a byproduct of England's own tumultuous past. As a religious site first and foremost, the Abbey was at the forefront of the religious unrest that occasionally swept the British Isles, whether it was Henry VIII's formation of the Church of England or his devoutly Catholic daughter earning the sobriquet Bloody Mary. As a result of it all, the Abbey has served different religious purposes over the course of time as well.

The Tower of London

Picture of the original entrance to the White Tower

The Tower of London is one of the most historic sites in all of England, and still one of the most popular. All around is the modern City of London, one of the world's most prosperous and power financial districts, but the Tower is still a daunting structure that looms across the landscape. Not a single structure but a vast network of medieval and early modern fortifications, it anchors the southeastern end of the old City and controls access to the River Thames and, through it, London's connection to the sea. While the both the City and the Thames are often obscured by the walls once visitors are inside the Tower, they are inextricably tied to the building, giving the Tower its entire reason for existence.

Even today, taking a tour of the Tower can seemingly bring its history to life. Inside the visitor center are replicas of a crown, an executioner's axe and similar artifacts, but for most visitors, this is just the start. After they cross a small courtyard and approach the first gate, known as the Middle Tower, they come to a stone bridge over a now-dry moat and enter the castle itself through the Byward Tower. The Tower, like many fortresses of its day, was built in concentric rings, so inside the outer wall is a narrow strip of land before the inner walls. Long, narrow buildings line the inside of the outer wall, and to the left along Mint Street these structures once housed the operation of the Royal Mint, making all of the coins of the realm.

From there, most visitors continue straight along, typically guided by one of the colorfully-dressed Yeoman Guards (the famous "Beefeaters"). Under the watch of the Bell Tower, they continue along the south face of the inner wall, on Water Lane, and just ahead is the famed Traitor's Gate; while today the area around here is paved and dry, in earlier times this was a "watergate" that allowed boats entry to the fortress. It was so named because this was the entrance by which prisoners (often traitors) entered the fortress, often never to leave. Ahead is Wakefield Tower, the entrance to the inner courtyards and a space that can be rented for small banquets and private dinners.

Inside the inner courtyards, visitors get a good first look at the White Tower, the 11th century Norman castle at the heart of the Tower (and the original "Tower" the entire complex is named for). Built of distinctive white stone, it has been a beacon of royal power for centuries. It is four stories tall and at points has walls of up to 15 feet thick, with towers on the four corners that have cupolas atop them (added much later than the original structure). Within the Tower is an impressive collection of medieval armor and arms, as well as the well-preserved St. John's Chapel. Directly behind the White Tower is the Waterloo Block, also known as the Jewel House. A perennial favorite of visitors, the Crown Jewels of the United Kingdom are stored here when not in use.

In the southeast corner of the inner courtyard (the "Inner Ward") is a charming green space backed by lovely Tudor structures whose calm belies their bloody history. This is the Tower Green which was the location of the executions of all of those prisoners who were given "Private" deaths (as opposed to a "Public" death which occurred outside the walls on Tower Hill before the London mob). It is perhaps best known as the site of the deaths of three of Henry

VIII's wives: Anne Boleyn, Catherine Howard, and Jane Grey. One of the surrounding buildings, the Queen's House, was named after its most famous prisoner - Anne Boleyn - but was also the site of the trial of the notorious Guy Fawkes.

Other sites within the walls of the Tower include the famous ravens (according to legend, if they ever leave the Tower the monarchy will fall), the museum of the Royal Regiment of Fusiliers (whose ceremonial commander is the Constable of the Tower) and the Ceremony of the Keys. The Ceremony is performed nightly by the Yeoman Warders when they seal the gates of the Tower and the Chief Warder passes the keys to the Resident Governor. Just beyond the Tower rises the great supports of the Tower Bridge (often confused with the smaller London Bridge) and the Thames.

Ultimately, it's impossible to fully appreciate the Tower without understanding its context. Like all fortresses, it was built to control and protect its surroundings, and the history of the Tower is bound up in the mutual histories of London and the Monarchy. The unfolding saga of war, imprisonment, glory, and treason in England can all be told through the lens of the Tower, and the lives that intersected with it.

Buckingham Palace

"We think of medieval England as being a place of unbelievable cruelty and darkness and superstition. We think of it as all being about fair maidens in castles, and witch-burning, and a belief that the world was flat. Yet all these things are wrong." - Terry Jones

"I'm glad we've been bombed. It makes me feel I can look the East End in the face." - The Queen Mother in 1940 after Buckingham Palace had been bombed by the Nazis

When people think of the British Royal family, and more specifically where they live, the first image that often pops into mind is that of stately Buckingham Palace, with its changing of the guard and the occasional royal coach leaving or entering. Others may think of the royal country estate of Windsor Castle, a favorite of both Britain's longest-reigning and second longest-reigning monarchs. And there was a time when both royal residences played second fiddle to a much better known home, the elegant Kensington Palace.

In his multi-volume work, *Old and New London* (1878), Edward Walford wrote, "It has often been said by foreigners that if they were to judge of the dignity and greatness of a country by the palace which its sovereign inhabits, they would not be able to ascribe to Her Majesty Queen Victoria that proud position among the 'crowned heads' of Europe which undoubtedly belongs to her. But though Buckingham Palace is far from being so magnificent as Versailles is, or the Tuilleries once were, yet it has about it an air of solidity and modest grandeur, which renders it no unworthy residence for a sovereign who cares more for a comfortable home than for display."

This is ultimately what palaces are all about: power and impressions. Buckingham Palace is not different, for though it was originally built as a home of a private citizen, once a king bought it, its future was sealed. Walford continued, "Indeed, it has often been said that, with the exception of St. James's, Buckingham Palace is the ugliest royal residence in Europe; and although vast sums of money have been spent at various times upon its improvement and embellishment, it is very far from being worthy of the purpose to which it is dedicated—lodging the sovereign of the most powerful monarchy in the world. It fronts the western end of St. James's Park, which here converges to a narrow point; the Mall, upon the north, and Birdcage Walk, upon the south, almost meeting before its gates."

While this was often true, fortunately it was just as often untrue, as men and women of high and low rank worked through the years, in times of life and death, and peace and war, to make it a home the British people could be proud of.

Big Ben

Big Ben is one of the most recognizable symbols of Britain, and indeed one of the most famous structures in the world. A quintessential part of London, every movie set in London features an establishing shot of Big Ben, and many guidebooks of London have the clock tower as its cover photo. London and Big Ben are forever linked in the consciousness of the Western world.

As it turns out, now is the time to admire and learn about Big Ben, because some believe it is likely to fall over. Since 2012, several sources have reported about the cracks appearing in walls all over the Palace of Westminster. This building houses Parliament and the House of Lords, which comprise the legislative bodies of the British Government. The building has stood in the same location since 1288, although it has not always been the same building. The palace and the tower have gone through renovation, rebuilding, fire, and more rebuilding, over the course of the last 720 years.

During the Battle of Britain in the Second World War, the clock tower was the only part of

Westminster Palace to merely sustain superficial damage, but as the Luftwaffe pummeled away at the city and the country, the chimes became a symbol of the resilience of the British people.[1] While the chimes have been stopped in the past due to mechanical error, the enemy was never able to silence Big Ben. This was a big part of the reason that England and the world continue to attach such significance to this clock tower.

Tower Bridge

A modern picture of Tower Bridge

"London Bridge is falling down,

Falling down, falling down

London Bridge is falling down,

My fair lady."

For most people, this playful child's rhyme conjures up visions of the tall, majestic, two-towered bridge spanning the River Thames near the Tower of London, with its high footpath providing one of the best views available of the city. The only problem is, this vision is wrong, for the London Bridge of modern times is neither tall nor majestic. Indeed, it is not at all memorable for any reason except for its ability to get the city's commuters back and forth to work each day.

In fact, the tall bridge that symbolizes not just the city but the nation is Tower Bridge, and while it is among the oldest major bridges in London, it is hardly the first to have been built on

[1] Peter MacDonald, *Big Ben: The Bell, the Clock and the Tower* (London: The History Press, 2013),

the Thames, or even on that spot. In actuality, the first men to build a bridge on that spot probably spoke Latin as their first language.

As time passed, technology changed, and with it, the nature of bridge building. Wood gave way to stone, which in turn gave way to iron and steel. At the same, London grew on both land and water, with more people living in and near the city, and more people plying the river in bigger and bigger ships. The people on land needed to get across the river, and the people on the river needed to be able to move along without too much interference. It was obvious that the city needed a new bridge, but years passed before the right design for one came along.

When it finally did, there were still other, non-practical concerns, specifically that the bridge fit in with its surrounding historical environment. In particular, this meant that Londoners wanted to ensure that the bridge's look fit in with the nearby Tower of London. Thus was born a bridge conceived within the marriage of need and desire, strength and beauty. Tower Bridge is unlikely to fall down, or even be torn down, anytime soon, but it is still worthy of singing about.

Westminster Abbey

Traditional Features of a Church

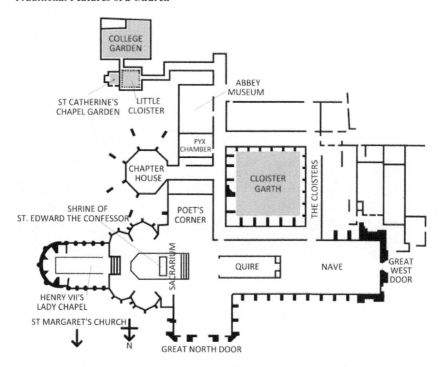

The current layout of Westminster Abbey

"I mean, you can't walk down the aisle in Westminster Abbey in a strapless dress, it just won't happen - it has to suit the grandeur of that aisle, it's enormous." – Bruce Oldfield

Nave: The long main body of the Church, in most Christian churches it is where the majority of the congregation sits in pews.

Herry Lawford's picture of the Nave

Aisle: A long passageway that runs alongside the nave, separated from this main area by a colonnade of columns. The ceilings of the aisle are often lower than that of the nave which has a clerestory above it.

Chancel: An area around and behind the principal altar which, in Westminster and many churches is topped by an apse. The chancel is considered to be sacred space and is often physically separated from the worshipper and accessible only by priests.

Clerestory: A row of windows, usually clear, set high up in the walls of the church, above the primary stained glass and the level of the aisle. The clerestory is designed to bring light into the sanctuary.

Font: A bowl on a pedestal, reminiscent of a large stone birdbath, where baptisms occur in traditions like Anglican Church where baptism is done on infants or small children. It often has its own side chapel.

Lectern: A stand on floor the level where a large copy of the Bible is held for use in readings during Mass. In Anglican churches like Westminster, it is often made of brass and shaped like a soaring eagle - the symbol of John the Evangelist.

Apse: An area behind the main altar of the church, usually a semi-circular domed area; it is separated from the Nave by the Transept.

Transept: If the main body of a traditional Cross-shaped Church like Westminster is the nave, the shorter piece that crosses it near the altar is the Transept. The transept often holds numerous side-chapels.

Choir/Quire: The area of a church where the choir and the clergy sit, separated from the main body of worshipers. In large traditional churches like Westminster, it is often located within the nave close to the transept and blocks the view of the altar of visitors entering the church.

THE CHOIR OF WESTMINSTER ABBEY, WITH NEW STALLS, SCREEN, &c.

A 19th century illustration of the choir

Pulpit: A raised stand or box, separated from the floor by a small flight of steps. This is where the presiding clergy member delivers the sermon. Before electronic amplification, they were designed to amplify the speaker's voice.

The Dark Ages and Origins of the Church

Like all ancient churches, the exact foundation and origins of Westminster Abbey is lost to the mists of time. Traditional legend holds that it was founded by Sebert, the King of the East Saxons, in 616 AD during the throes of his people's conversion to Christianity. Sebert (sometimes spelled "Saberht") was said to have also founded the original St. Paul's downriver in London. Much older churches than this are not to be found in England because the Saxon invaders were worshippers of the old Norse/Germanic gods and were thus considered the scourges of the Christians. Sebert was the first Christian king of his people, so any churches from the Roman period (and they would have been relatively few considering the marginal position and early fall of Roman Britain) did not survive into the Saxon period.[2]

Sebert chose a place several miles upriver from the existing site of the City of London on an island called the Isle of Thorney. The name "westminster" is a simple one: "west" for the direction from London, and "minster" being an Old English term for a monastery. According to legend, St. Peter miraculously appeared to consecrate the newly completed church, which has since been dedicated to him.[3]

That said, there is no written or archaeological evidence to corroborate the foundation of Westminster Abbey during Sebert's reign. The primary historian of the Saxon period, the Venerable Bede (672-735), wrote during the early 700s but never mentioned the church, and while that does not necessarily preclude its existence, a church with a royal foundation would have been an important site at the time.

The first hard, datable evidence associated with the building is a charter for a monastery named Westminster (and differentiated specifically from St. Paul's) granted by King Offa of Mercia (757-796) in 785. Other early dates for the church come from a 10th century charter granted by King Edgar the Peaceful of Wessex (943-975), in which the territories controlled by the monastery are more clearly delineated. Additionally, there is a traditional date of 960; according to the historian William of Malmesbury (1095-1143), St. Dunstan (909-988) brought 12 Benedictine monks to the monastery from the ancient monastic seat of Glastonbury and expanded the existing monastery. However, while Westminster definitely emerged as a major seat of the Order of St. Benedict, the story of St. Dunstan has as little corroboration as the original foundation by King Sebert three centuries earlier.

---

2   "Westminster Abbey" at *The Encyclopedia Britannica.* Accessed online at:
    http://www.britannica.com/EBchecked/topic/641068/Westminster-Abbey
3   "Westminster Abbey" at *The New Catholic Encyclopedia.* Accessed online at:
    http://www.newadvent.org/cathen/15598a.htm

Unfortunately, scholars cannot consult archaeological evidence for help because the exact site of the original monastic structure has been lost, and wherever it was, it has been undoubtedly buried by construction over several centuries.

Edward the Confessor and Westminster Abbey

Kjetil Bjørnsrud's picture of Edward's Throne

Medieval depiction of Edward the Confessor

There is no figure more important to the history of Westminster Abbey, no individual who shaped its destiny and identity, more than Saint/King Edward "the Confessor" of the House of Wessex, who ruled as king of a united England from 1033-1065. The last universally recognized king of his line[4] before the Norman Conquest, Edward set the stage for the Normans and has served as a symbol of unity with the Saxon past ever since. Ironically, for a king so closely associated with Westminster, it might come as a surprise that Edward did not have his coronation at Westminster but instead at Winchester Cathedral, a major ecclesiastical site during that era. In fact, Edward was the last king in English history up until the present day who did not have his coronation in Westminster.

Edward had a tumultuous reign, and as a child he was forced into exile by Norse conquests. Edward hid in Normandy, where his family had holdings, and during this period abroad, the young king took an oath to make a pilgrimage to Rome if he was reinstated to his throne. Upon his success, he appealed to the Pope to absolve him of this vow, but while the Pope did so, he did not let Edward completely off the hook because he insisted that the English king build a magnificent church dedicated to St. Peter. This was undoubtedly a canny move on the part of the Pope, because the king was unlikely to leave a realm he had just retaken regardless of his oaths, and a pilgrimage was of little benefit to Rome anyway. However, the proposed church would be

---

4   Harold, often considered the last Saxon king, who lost to William at the Battle of Hastings (1066) had not completely consolidated his reign by the time he died.

richly endowed and a jewel of the Roman Catholic Church, and if its loyalty to the Vatican was ever in doubt, its dedication to St. Peter (of whom the Pope was seen as the direct spiritual descendant) confirmed its place in the Roman camp. This loyalty was of importance to the Vatican at the time because of the recent 1054 schism with the Patriarch of Constantinople, a division that would eventually lead to the foundation of the Roman Catholic and Eastern Orthodox churches.

The King apparently agreed to the project with enthusiasm, likely because it fit within a larger plan of his own to create a grand royal compound as part of a new capital for himself. Kings in the Dark Ages were somewhat itinerant figures without fixed capitals due to the need to move from stronghold to stronghold as the needs of politics, war, or the king's whims dictated. To a degree, the king and his court were firefighters who had to travel and put down problems as they arose, all while trying to maintain the loyalty of often-rebellious barons. However, Edward sought to create a center of royal power from which he could rule over his kingdoms. The ancient rights of the City of London prevented him from making it his center of power and so he instead chose the nearby monastery of Westminster, conveniently outside of London but close enough to easily access its markets, moneylenders and similar services. The fact that the abbot of Westminster at the time, Edwin, was a close friend of the King's and that the church was already dedicated to St. Peter only sealed the deal.

At Westminster, the king sought to create not only a magnificent church but also a new palace, both in a matching Romanesque style. The Palace of Westminster became the seat of government housing the royal court, as well as the House of Lords and the House of Commons. From that point on, Westminster Abbey has been fundamentally tied to the Crown and the English (and then British) government. This, perhaps more than any other act, defined Westminster as the royal church of England, set apart from the more purely religious seats of Canterbury and York.

Work began on the structure, the first Romanesque church on the island of Britain, in 1055 and was pretty much complete in 1065, so Edward was able to attend its consecration a few days before his death. Edward would eventually be buried within the church that he had sponsored, the first of many tombs within the grounds, but the church was then caught up in the drama immediately succeeding Edward's death. There was a struggle for power which eventually led to an invasion by French-speaking Normans from the continent, a conflict that culminated in the Battle of Hastings (1066). At the battle, the Saxon heir to Edward's throne, King Harold, was killed during his army's defeat at the hands of William the Conqueror's invaders.

For his coronation, William traveled to Westminster and held the ceremony, thus beginning a tradition that every English and British monarch has followed since. However, while today this ritual is done to honor the traditions of the monarchy and its connection to St. Edward the Confessor, it was probably not out of profound respect that William chose the location. Like Edward, he could have chosen any convenient cathedral for the ritual, but he seems to have chosen Westminster as a manifestation of his triumph. After all, there was no greater symbol of the victory of the Normans over the Saxons than to crown their new king in the brand-new symbol of royal Saxon power. At the same time, the fact that William claimed to be Edward's true heir (which is how he legitimized the Conquest) meant he could also say that a coronation in his predecessor's church was a rightful inheritance. One must also remember that despite the newness of the church building, the foundation of the monastery dated back four centuries at this point and was thus a place imbued with antiquity and connection to the earliest days of Saxon Christianity.

An English coin depicting William the Conqueror

This is the Bayeux Tapestry's depiction of the Church at the time of Edward's death.

Henry III and the Current Construction

Medieval illustration depicting Richard II's marriage to Anne of Bohemia in 1382

For the next two centuries after the Norman Conquest, Westminster served admirably as the preeminent royal church for the realm, but there were some changes as construction on an expanded nave began in 1110 and lasted until 1163. As the 13th century dawned, another expansion was planned, and the small eastern semi-circular chapel behind the high altar was demolished and replaced with a larger lady chapel dedicated to the Virgin and consecrated in 1220. Both of these expansions were linked to the growing status of Edward the Confessor; like many Christian kingdoms, there was a tradition in Christian Saxon Britain of popular cults to deceased members of the royal family (who were treated as saints). While these cults were widespread in their day, none of these saints was officially recognized by the Catholic Church, and eventually the piety of the followers waned and they were largely forgotten. The exception to this was Edward the Confessor.

On the face of it, Edward was not a particularly likely candidate for canonization. He was famed for his violent temper, not to mention his love of war and the blood sport of hunting, all of which was frowned upon for saints. Moreover, while he had founded or built ecclesiastical structures like Westminster, this was standard behavior for Christian kings. However, it appears that popular veneration for St. Edward began almost immediately after his death, and since Westminster was the site of his relics, it quickly became a site of pilgrimage.

Understandably, official response to this cult was mixed. On the one hand, the early Norman kings were understandably leery of the veneration of a Saxon king because it could provide a potential rallying point for rebellion. On the other hand, the relics and interpretation of the cult was firmly within royal control rather than located in a distant province, and William the Conqueror had claimed descent from St. Edward as well. Thanks to that claim, the English monarchy stood to benefit from having a saintly connection.

Furthermore, English leaders understood that saints were big business in the Middle Ages, and the income from pilgrims was a major source of income for the monks of Westminster. This extra source of income was independent of royal patronage, which therefore gave them a freer hand and undoubtedly made them warmer to the possibility of Edward's canonization. Along with that, their position so close to the seat of royal power gave them added influence.

In the end, the Norman monarchs came to embrace St. Edward the Confessor, and the expansion of the nave of Westminster was the first expression of this. Edward's body was moved from whatever tomb it was kept in and placed alongside the High Altar where he was venerated, eventually pushing St. Peter, the official patron, out of the limelight. The reconstruction of the lady chapel likewise gave more space for pilgrims and worship behind the Altar, in an area with excellent views of the Saint's tomb.

As time went on, these initial expansions were viewed as insufficient, so a grand plan for reconstruction was hatched in the 13th century. Starting in 1245, under the abbots Richard Crokesley and Richard Ware and the patronage of King Henry III, the entire eastern portion of the church, including half of the nave, was demolished and completely rebuilt. For 30 years, construction continued apace until a series of disasters: the death of Henry in 1272; a terrible fire in 1298 which necessitated the reconstruction of the entire monastic complex; and the 1349 arrival of the Black Death, which devastated England as a whole and the monastic community specifically. These successive disasters led to a cessation of building for close to a century, so the nave was not completed until 1517, thanks to a boost of support under a new patron: Henry VII. This new King Henry also funded a reconstruction of the Lady Chapel which is today called the "Henry VII Lady Chapel." Henry was buried in this chapel after his death in 1509.

The effigy of Henry III in Westminster Abbey

The tomb of Henry III in Westminster Abbey

Portrait of Henry VII

Henry VII's burial was part of a general enthusiasm for monarchs to be buried within the Abbey's walls, and visitors to Westminster today are often surprised at how many people are buried within what is ostensibly a church, not an indoor cemetery or even an official national pantheon[5]. It is not even officially a royal tomb in the way many dynasties have a custom-built tomb for their royals, including el Escorial in Spain, Mauna 'Ala (the Royal Mausoleum of Hawai'i) and the Habsburg Imperial Crypt in Vienna. Westminster is not like any of these places, but it is a church where successive generations of monarchs and other prominent figures

---

5   Many nations, such as France, have a "pantheon," a temple-like structure which is built to house the remains of
    the nation's most illustrious figures.

have decided to be buried.

Much of the reason for this is the presence of St. Edward's relics. In the traditions of the Catholic Church, the bodies of saints are considered to contain some residue of the holiness that the man or woman possessed in life. As such, proximity to these relics conveyed some of that holy power to the everyday person. This was the reason for pilgrimage but also for the burial of the dead close to the bodies of the saint. The closer the proximity of the person to the saint, the stronger this influence was believed to be[6].

The new Church was also of a new style. The old Romanesque style was notable for its thick, short columns, its dark and small interiors, and its imperfect mimicry of old Roman styles (hence the description Romanesque). However, the new style was named for the people who first developed it: the Goths of today's France. The Gothic architecture was pioneered in French cathedrals in places like Chartres, but it also quickly became an international style that was enthusiastically adopted across the Western Christian world.

The Gothic style used pointed arches instead of the old rounded ones, as well as a technique called the "flying buttress," a support on the outer surface of the building onto which some of the stresses of holding up the outer walls can be distributed. This reconfiguring of the building's structure allowed for supports to become slimmer, further apart and fewer, which opened up unprecedented amounts of wall space for windows. This led in turn to a fluorescence of the art of stained glass. Great open walls of stained glass characterize Gothic churches, making them into glorious temples of light, all of which would have awed people of the time even more than they do for modern visitors[7].

6   *The Cult of the Saints: Its Rise and Function in Latin Christianity* by Peter Brown (1982)
7   "Gothic Architecture" in *The Encyclopedia Britannica.* Accessed online at:
    http://www.britannica.com/EBchecked/topic/239678/Gothic-architecture

Artificial light is used to draw attention to the flying buttresses.

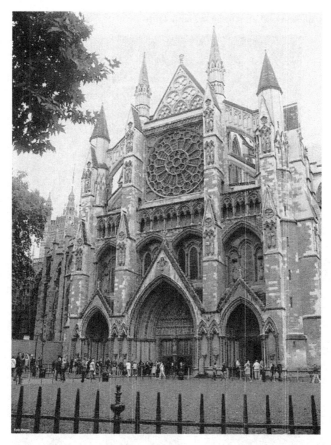

The Gothic influences on the North façade can be seen in this picture by Zachi Evenor.

Westminster was also a site of great temporal power since the Abbot of Westminster sat on the House of Lords, giving him influence over the affairs of the realm on par with the most important lords. Locally, the Abbot was considered a feudal lord who controlled the surrounding villages and countryside, which gave him both political and economic influence. As mentioned above, the steady flow of pilgrims and royal patronage also bolstered the Abbey's coffers and influence. All of this considerable influence elicited envy, distrust and bitterness that would eventually legitimize the next era in the Abbey's history: the dissolution of the monasteries.

Tudor Dissolution and an Abbey in Name Only

Portrait of Henry VIII

The dissolution of the Monasteries was one part of the much larger English Reformation. It is perhaps easy to over-simplify the Reformation by claiming that it was motivated by the English King Henry VIII's desire to divorce his various wives and remarry, but rarely does any king have the power to effect such overwhelming social change without at least some backing from the society at large. Even if Henry VIII had been able to break with the Catholic Church based solely upon his own desires, it was an innovation that would never have been able to live beyond his death.

Instead, while the desire to divorce may have been Henry's stated goal, it was a pretext. The dynasty to which Henry belonged - the Tudors - had been the victors of a vicious civil war called the War of the Roses, which was fought from 1455-1487. The kings that emerged out of that conflict were dedicated to creating a centralized state in which the monarch had tremendous power and which would hopefully avoid such conflicts in the future. As a result, the Tudor centralization affected all parts of civil governance and also extended into the realm of religion. What the Tudors did by breaking with the Catholic Church in Rome was to eliminate their greatest rival to power: the autonomous church. The wealthy priestly hierarchy would no longer be answerable to the Pope but instead to the monarch. Moreover, if the equally autonomous monastic establishments could be eliminated at the same time, then the monarch could redistribute their wealth by taking the best gems for himself (as he would with Westminster) and giving away the rest to loyal noble families, further bolstering his rule. Henry VIII correctly bargained that these families - flush with new power - would be willing to support the monarchy against any potential return of the Catholic Church (which would presumably seek to re-establish the monasteries).

At the same time that these political and economic considerations influenced Henry, there was also a new theological trend that would justify his changes: Protestantism. Henry does not appear to have been deeply influenced by Protestant theology himself (he had previously been the "Defender of the Faith" for the Pope), but he certainly used the strength of its followers. The Protestant Reformation had spread across Europe in response to the corruption, wealth and inordinate influence of the Catholic Church, and while their hatred might have been strongest towards the Pope, nowhere in Britain itself was their ire raised as it was toward the monks of the great monastic establishments like Westminster, St. Paul's and Glastonbury. Protestants looked at the centuries of treasures these places had accumulated as a cancer upon the true Christian faith.

Another impact of the Protestant Reformation was the de-emphasis placed upon the role of saints in worship. The new Anglican Church developed a complex and at times contradictory relationship with the concept of saints; while they recognized that saints did exist and were humans worthy of respect and imitation, they did not believe saints were worthy of veneration and prayer. Thus, saintly statues were removed from throughout Westminster (especially the exterior facade), as were many traditional decorations due to the fact the Protestants favored an austere decor that did not distract from the ceremony. In the vast majority of churches, saintly relics were either hidden or (more commonly) removed and destroyed, but in Westminster, St. Edward the Confessor's body remained in its place near the altar, providing yet one more reason why Westminster is distinct. This may have been due to royal protection or the fact that Edward the Confessor was considered a monarch within the traditional mausoleum of the royal family. One unintended impact of the removal of the saintly statues is that it freed up considerable space on walls and inside chapels, thereby providing more room for tombs and the commemorations of the deceased. This has certainly helped give Westminster its modern feel as a gigantic mausoleum.

Hence, when Henry VIII broke with Rome and dissolved the monasteries, he found a strong following among his allies in the nobility and among the growing number of dissidents in the Protestant faction. While monastic lands and wealth elsewhere were given to noble houses or to cathedrals under the control of loyal bishops, in Westminster, the king decided to exert his power personally. The abbots of Westminster had long been a powerful force at both the regional and national level, but the king moved to consolidate that power for himself. Thus, in 1539, Westminster Abbey was technically dissolved, and in its place, Henry created an institution called a Royal Peculiar. Westminster Abbey was not a cathedral (and it is not today), and there was no Bishop appointed to rival the great bishops of London, Canterbury or York; instead, the organization created in the time of Henry VIII - more or less still in place today - was a "Collegiate Church." The governing body is a group of clergy called a "College," the members are called " Prebendaries" ("Prebend" in singular), and they are led by an individual called the "Dean." The modern educational terms "college" and "dean" come from these institutions, which were at the heart of the original Oxford and Cambridge Universities. These priests are typically chosen from the most respected parish priests and Church administrators from the surrounding region and may or may actually preside over services at Westminster, though day-to-day religious services are generally conducted by younger, lower-ranking priests. Together, the Deacons are called the "Chapter" (akin to a Board of Directors), and they meet in the heart of the old Abbey: the Chapterhouse. In addition to Westminster, this Collegiate Church system is found in most Church of England cathedrals in Britain.

Westminster Abbey has been controlled since 1539 by the Church of England (the "C of E" to most Britons). Also called the "Anglican" or "Episcopal" Church, the Church of England has retained a unique position in Christianity because it bridges the Protestant and Catholic worlds. Anglicans are Protestant because they reject the control of the Pope, but they are Catholic because they view their priests as having a direct spiritual lineage from the Twelve Apostles and they practice the Mass. Throughout the history of England since 1539, there have been tensions between these two poles of Christian worship, and those tensions have led to bloodshed on numerous occasions.

Westminster Abbey today is very much a product of this complex history, and the impacts of it can be seen woven into the ritual, administration, art and modern uses of the building. At least in theory, the Collegiate Church preserves some of the democratic governance of the old monastic system, but in Westminster, this autonomy is greatly constrained by its position as a Royal Peculiar, which means appointment to the priestly positions from Dean on down is not done through the normal channels of the Church hierarchy but instead by the direct hand of the monarch. In essence, the Royal Peculiar of Westminster Abbey is treated in law as a private chapel serving the needs of the monarch, much in the way that local nobility throughout England traditionally had the prerogative to appoint the chaplains of their private chapels.

While Westminster "belongs" to the monarchy, the running of the institution is handled by the Dean, who inherited many of the powers of the old Abbot. Between 1585 and 1900, the Abbey (through the Dean's administration) controlled lands of the local City of Westminster and the surrounding countryside known as the Liberty of Westminster. In 1900, these powers were at least officially secularized by being transferred to a new institution called the Westminster Court of Burgesses, which was led by the High Steward of Westminster (today a ceremonial position appointed for life by the Dean and Chapter[8]).

The Abbey was a Cathedral with a bishop for a short period of time under Henry VIII. From 1540-1550, there was a Bishop of Westminster, followed by a period until 1556 when it was the co-seat along with St. Paul's of the Bishop of London. However, this was the general solution that Henry had given to all of the great Abbey Churches until he found more permanent uses for them. Likewise, there was a short-lived period under his daughter Elizabeth I when the monks were re-established and the Abbot of Westminster was the last monastic to sit on the House of Lords. However, after this period of uncertainty, the pattern of governance and worship was established at Westminster that remained continuous until the modern age.

---

8   http://www.westminster-abbey.org/press/news/news/2011/february/lord-luce-appointed-high-steward-of-westminster-abbey

Effigy of Elizabeth I in Westminster Abbey

Foundations of the Modern Church

"I should like to have seen a gallery of coronation beauties, at Westminster Abbey, confronted for a moment by this band of Island girls; their stiffness, formality, and affectation contrasted with the artless vivacity and unconcealed natural graces of these savage maidens. It would be the Venus de' Medici placed beside a milliner's doll." – Herman Melville

The final addition to the modern Abbey was the construction of the two large towers over the Great West Door in 1722. Since that time, the Abbey has mostly kept the same appearance. However, this similarity of appearance belies the major changes in use that the Abbey went through during this period.

Gordon Joly's picture of the Great West Door

One element of change was that during this period, the lands controlled by Westminster were completely absorbed into the urban conurbation of Greater London, although official control of civic affairs by the Dean and Chapter would not be removed until 1900. This absorption was one element of the Abbey's shift from being essentially an organ of government with ceremonies largely meeting the private needs of the rulers into a site for direct engagement between the government and the governed.

In addition, another development was the increasing use of burial at the Abbey as a reward for service to the nation by commoners, which occurred around the same time that the practice of royal burial ceased in 1760. Royals were joined by scientists like Sir Isaac Newton (1727),

Charles Lyell (1875), Charles Darwin (1882), and David Livingstone (1873), as well as men of letters like Robert Browning (1889), Charles Dickens (1870), Alfred Lord Tennyson (1892) and Dr. Samuel Johnson (1784). The death and interment of each of these individuals (and many others) became a national ceremony that symbolically tied the life of the individual to the nation, the state and the monarchy.

The tomb of Sir Isaac Newton

In 1725, King George I created a new honorific knightly society, the Order of the Bath. Named for a medieval tradition of giving knights a ritual purification bath akin to an adult baptism, the Order of the Bath was essentially a new organization. Its purpose was to recognize great accomplishments amongst members of the military and, to a lesser extent, the public administration. Since a reorganization of the Order in 1825, the official chapel of the Order has been the Henry VII Lady Chapel, and today the Order's banners decorate the chapel alongside seats for the 34 senior-most members of the organization[9].

Westminster Abbey with a procession of Knights of the Bath, by Canaletto (1749)

The reorganization transformed the order from a pseudo-medieval military society (with a small number of knights expected to undergo prayer vigils and coordinate the defense of the realm) to a much larger honorary society meant to reward the service of Britain's military men. The movement to the large Henry VII Chapel was part of a general conversion of Westminster Abbey during the 18th and 19th centuries into a ceremonial centerpiece for the public rituals of the monarchy, essentially a set for propaganda pageantry.

---

9   "Order of the Bath" at *The Official Website of the British Monarchy.* Accessed online at: http://www.royal.gov.uk/MonarchUK/Honours/OrderoftheBath.aspx

Nowhere was this more evident than in the evolution of the coronation ceremony. During this period, especially in the 19th century, the British government developed the essence of the modern coronation at Westminster. While there are definitely continuities between the modern ceremony and its medieval predecessors, there has actually been a major sea-change in ritual from the Victorian Period onwards. Before the 19th century, Britain was one of many monarchies in Europe vying for prestige, and one way that the British set themselves apart from the Catholic monarchies of France and Spain was by having restrained, simple ceremonies for events like coronations and royal weddings. During the Protestant Reformation (1539) and the French Revolution (1789), the British prided themselves on the rationality and simplicity of these rites, which were essentially family affairs for the Royal Family and the high nobility. However, after the French Revolution, Britain was no longer on the forefront of rationality and modernity but merely a stalwart of the old royal order. The bolstering of the legitimacy of the monarchy to the masses became a primary concern (some might even say an obsession) for the government after the Revolution in Paris and the death of Louis XVIII, so one tool they used for doing this was a massive uptick in the complexity, cost and importance of royal ceremonials. Innovations like open carriage rides through the streets for the new monarch or the newlywed royals, increased numbers of spectators, participation of the press, and now radio and television commentary of the proceedings were all essentially propaganda tools used to bolster the legitimacy of the institution of the monarchy[10]. Westminster, with its antiquity, beauty, and grand size, has served as the central stage for all of this pageantry, giving another new political role to the ancient building.

---

10 *The Invention of Tradition* by Eric Hobsbawm and Terence Ranger (1992)

The Abbey in the 20th and 21st Centuries

Statues for the 20th century Christian martyrs commemorated at the Abbey

The fundamental roles of the modern Abbey were well established by the dawn of the 20th century, so it's only natural that the last 115 years have not been years of great innovation or change for the institution. This is fitting in a sense because the Abbey has come to represent continuity and tradition, and many Britons take comfort in the stalwart nature of institutions like it.

Meanwhile, the official hierarchy and institutions of the Tudor Royal Peculiar have lost much of their direct administrative power. For instance, the High Steward of Westminster no longer manages the civic government of the Borough of Westminster but is instead merely a ceremonial position and a prominent steppingstone for those moving up in the still-overlapping hierarchies of Church and State.[11]

Fortunately, Westminster does not bear the scars of the World Wars that some areas of London

---

11 https://www.churchofengland.org/media-centre/news/2012/04/archbishopric-of-canterbury-chair-of-crown-nominations-commission-appointed.aspx

and greater England suffered, due mostly to the fact that the Abbey (and its delicate stained glass) is located alongside the center of the British government, placing it within the most fiercely protected area of airspace in the entire country. During the Battle of Britain, the treasures of the church were sent to safe locations in the north, while the toms were covered in sandbags for their protection. While St. Paul's to the east was at times wreathed in smoke and flame, Westminster was spared most of this destruction, though the Abbey was home to a group of volunteers who slept in the Nave every night with firefighting equipment in order to put out any incendiary bombs that happened to make their way into the structure. One set of incendiary bombs did penetrate during German attacks, but the damage was minimal. The Abbey was also the site of the official state prayer on VE Day (the day Germany surrendered), with roughly 25,000 attendees[12].

Westminster is still legally a Royal Peculiar and serves foremost the needs of the Royal Family. The first time the world at large really got a good look at Westminster was for the coronation of Elizabeth II in 1953, the first British royal coronation ceremony to be filmed for television and a major cultural milestone not only in Britain but throughout the world. The soaring backdrop of Westminster, redolent in antiquity and bursting with the elite of the dying British Empire, made an impression on all who watched the proceedings.

While there have been no royal burials in Westminster since George in 1760 - today the royal family entombs its dead in the roomier confines of Windsor Castle - it has continued to serve for the far more joyous occasions of royal weddings. Weddings occurred here infrequently during the Middle Ages, especially in the 1200s, but between 1382 and 1919, there were no royal weddings in Westminster. In 1919, however, Westminster again became the principal site for royal unions, perhaps the most important new development in the 20th century history of the Abbey. There have been 10 such wedding since then,[13] and the most important of these were the ceremonies for heirs, including the marriage of Princess (now Queen) Elizabeth to Philip, Duke of Edinburgh in 1947, and the marriage of Prince William to Kate Middleton in 2011[14]. In both of these events, Westminster served as the stage for royal pageantry, dramatic photos, and general national pride Britain.

The Abbey Church has also been the site of numerous funerals, including all of the hundreds of individuals interred at the site. In recent years, there have also been state funerals for individuals who were not interred there, including Queen Elizabeth (the "Queen Mother"), Diana, Princess of Wales, and Queen Alexandra (wife of King Edward VII). The funeral of Princess Diana in particular was an event of international scope equal to that of the most important weddings and coronations.

---

12 "History: War Damage" http://www.westminster-abbey.org/our-history/war-damage
13 As well as four more in the medieval period.
14 The wedding of Prince Charles to Lady Diana Spencer in 1981 was held in St. Paul's Cathedral.

Tour of the Church

"As I passed along the side walls of Westminster Abbey, I hardly saw any thing but marble monuments of great admirals, but which were all too much loaded with finery and ornaments, to make on me at least, the intended impression." – Karl Philipp Moritz

Although it is not London's largest church, an honor goes to the mighty St. Paul's in the old City of London, the Abbey is an undoubtedly impressive structure. The giant Abbey is 531 feet (162 meters) long, and at its widest point (the transept) it is 203 feet (62 meters) wide. The space under the nave and transept is roughly 80 feet (24 meters) across. The main building stands 102 feet (31 meters) high, and the tops of the two towers above the great gate are 225 feet (69 meters) tall. Overall, when viewed from above, the building takes the form of a Latin Cross (a simple cross with a longer lower part and a single crosspiece)[15]. This type of form is not uncommon amongst the great churches of the Latin Christian tradition[16] and is the church shape that is generally pictured when people imagine a cathedral.

---

15 "Westminster Abbey" at *How Stuff Works* accessed online at:
   http://geography.howstuffworks.com/europe/westminster-abbey.htm
16 Which includes both Roman Catholicism - the Church that built Westminster - and also Anglicanism, the Church that has worshipped in the structure for the majority of its history

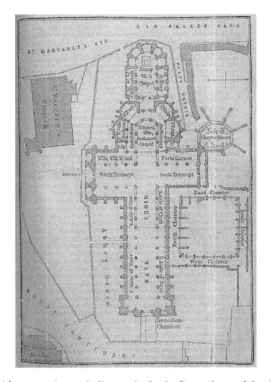

This 19th century layout indicates the Latin Cross shape of the Abbey.

Visitors to the church generally approach the structure from the west, in the large open courtyard that surrounds the structure. They are advised that the Abbey is not a museum or a monument but first and foremost a working Church, so during the multiple daily ceremonies, they are asked to respect the sacred proceedings and not make unnecessary noise. That said, visitors are also invited to participate in the ceremonies, and many who are not even Christian do so in order to enjoy the music (pipe organs and boys choirs) and ceremonials of the ancient rituals of Mass and Evensong which have occurred here daily for over a millennium. Indeed, it is one of the most ancient halls of Christian worship in the British Isles[17].

Great West Door

Flanked by two mighty towers, the Great West Door is a truly impressive entryway. The front facade of the structure is worth looking at in itself. One knows that this building is a product of the Protestant Reformation due to the fact that all along the exterior are niches that once held

17 *Westminster Abbey Homepage.* Accessed online at: http://www.westminster-abbey.org/

statues of saints which were removed by the more zealous Reformers. While the statues are gone, the niches remain as a reminder of this "iconoclastic[18]" period of Church history. Today it is here that visitors purchase tickets and buy souvenirs before entering.

The Great West Door

The Nave

Upon entering the Abbey, visitors encounter the Nave, the long main body of the church which was completely rebuilt in the 13th century with the then-cutting edge Gothic style. As a result, the walls are high and made up of a forest of arches with pointed tops and seemingly countless stained glass windows. Stained glass was a distinctive characteristic of the Gothic style, and the windows in the Abbey bathe the interior spaces of places like the Nave with beautiful colored light and illuminating Bible stories, lives of saints, and similar pious images for the illiterate faithful.[19]

---

18 This term means "icon-breaking" and in its original form meant a religious movement that destroyed the images of saints or gods as they saw them as heretical. Many strongly Protestant faiths are fiercely iconoclastic, as is the Sunni Muslim tradition, especially in the modern Wahhabi sect.
19 "Westminster Abbey" at *The New Catholic Encyclopedia.* Accessed online at: http://www.newadvent.org/cathen/15598a.htm

Many would agree that the best time to enter the Nave is during one of the regular performances of the pipe organs. Installed for the coronation of King George VI in 1937, it is only the latest of a series of ever-grander organs dating back to at least 1304. Like all of the great Gothic churches, Westminster was designed with an organ in mind, and the building is essentially part of the instrument. The stones of the grand hall resound with the organ's music, which appears to come from nowhere and everywhere as the walls themselves vibrate. The music penetrates and, if performed the way it is intended, enhances the spiritual power of the structure. The list of official Organists of Westminster Abbey, an old position in the hierarchy, has included some of the finest musicians in English history, including the masterful John Blow and Henry Purcell. Even today, the Summer Organ Festival brings the modern masters together in the old Abbey Church[20].

Although the Nave is one of the outermost areas of the Abbey, visitors can't help but notice the large number of tombs and memorials covering the walls and floors. The Royals are clustered closer to the High Altar, but in the Nave, the most famous of these tombs is that of Sir Isaac Newton. This tomb includes a statue of the great physicist with the implements of his trade: books, a globe, and an apple[21].

Quire

The Quire ("Choir" in American English) is a place where the great antiquity of Westminster first begins to confront most visitors. The Nave is awe-inspiring, but the wooden quire stalls, used by centuries of choirboys, priests, and dignitaries, are full of history.[22] The quire is akin to a wooden building without a ceiling that is set in the center of the nave, and the structure has two entry archways: one facing the High Altar and the other facing the Great West Door. This means that during formal ceremonies (everything from Easter to a Royal Wedding), groups of priests and worshippers can proceed along the nave all the way to the Altar. On both sides of the central processual aisle are several rows of beautiful, hand carved wooden seats. The highest seats have tall backs that meld into the woodwork of the walls, all of which are topped by the medieval banners of the Order of Bath. During ceremonies, the lower seats of the choir - those closest to the aisle - are filled with red and white robed choirboys. In everyday events like the nightly Evensong, the rest of the choir seats are filled with worshipers, but during rituals of national importance, they fill up with bishops and other church dignitaries.

Cloisters and the Cloister Garden

---

20 "Music and the Choir: The Organ" at the homepage of *Westminster Abbey* accessed online at: http://www.westminster-abbey.org/music/organ

21 "History: Sir Isaac Newton" at the homepage of *Westminster Abbey* accessed online at: http://www.westminster-abbey.org/our-history/people/david-livingstone

22 "Westminster Abbey" at *The Encyclopedia Britannica.* Accessed online at: http://www.britannica.com/EBchecked/topic/641068/Westminster-Abbey

Bernard Gagnon's picture of the cloister

Those seeking a full tour of the Abbey should duck out of the main sanctuary at this time and exit the building through one of several doors on the southern side. These lead to the rooms of the old monastic compound, today used primarily for administrative purposes. It has both above-ground and subterranean rooms available for visitors to view.

While the monks and Abbots are long gone - victims of the Protestant Reformation in 1539 - there are many reminders of their life in this area of the complex, especially the cloister garden. The "cloister" was the area of the monastery that was off-limits to all but the monks and their invited guests, and at the center of it is a square courtyard with a center of grass and plants that is surrounded by a raised stone walkway with a roof supported by columns (a "colonnade"). The monks would circumnavigate the courtyard in a form of mobile prayer and contemplation that many found useful for communion with God. In the Middle Ages, this was a place of escape and respite from the hustle and bustle of the Abbey church, and it remains an oasis even today.[23]

Abbey Museum and the Pyx Chamber

---

23 "Westminster Abbey (The Collegiate Church of St Peter)" in the *National Heritage List for England.* On the homepage of English Heritage. Accessed online at: http://list.english-heritage.org.uk/resultsingle.aspx?uid=1291494

Beyond the cloister garden and further into the old monastic structures are two rooms that might attract the interest of tourists: the Abbey Museum and the Pyx Chamber. Both of these are located in historic monastic rooms, but there is little evidence of the monks here.

The Abbey Museum is remarkable because it holds the treasures of Westminster. The modern museum is located in the "undercroft," a subterranean area that was a storage facility in the medieval monastery, and it includes objects like effigies made of the royal dead, other funerary items, stained glass, a rare original statue of St. Peter, and altarpieces. The lack of gold and silver objects is largely due to the fact that many such medieval objects were considered to be too "popish" (Catholic) in the Reformation and were thus destroyed. Furthermore, despite the Abbey's connection with coronations, the Crown Jewels are not held in this location but are instead kept under protected lock and key in the Tower of London in the old City of London downriver[24].

Picture of an empty effigy in the Abbey

Next to the Abbey Museum is the Pyx Chamber. The Pyx is a container (often in the form of a

24 "Visiting the Abbey: The Museum" at the *Westminster Abbey Homepage.* Accessed online at: http://www.westminster-abbey.org/visit-us/highlights/the-museum

call made of precious metals) which was traditionally suspended on chains above the High Altar along with a lit candle in its interior. This device was used in the Middle Ages and continues to be used in Catholic churches and in some highly traditionalist Anglican settings. It is used to hold the Host (blessed Communion wafers) between Mass, and the priest could draw upon this supply of wafers when traveling to visit the homes of the sick and invalid who could not physically attend Church but were still able to enjoy the benefits of Holy Communion.

The pyxes on display at the Abbey served another use. They were similar boxes, but they were created to house coins which were stored for an annual trial during which royal officials tested the coins for their purity of gold and silver. However, the minting and testing of the coins was done not by Church officials; instead, the Exchequer produced the coins and a city guild called the Worshipful Company of Goldsmiths tested them. It is an example of the deep intersection between church and state in the United Kingdom[25].

While the Pyx Chamber is often overlooked by modern visitors to the Church, the pyx as a religious implement (rather than one of measuring coinage) has long been a spot for rancorous debate in the Anglican Church. Today, and for many centuries now, the Church is divided between those who view Mass as a symbolic ritual meant to assist prayer (the "Low" Church, those with more Protestant tendencies) and those who see the Mass as a miraculous event where the Host becomes literally imbued with the essence of Christ (the "High" Church, those with more Catholic tendencies). This debate, while it seems rather silly to many even within the Church today, was one of the theological sources of the Great Schism within the Anglican Church that led to the English Civil Wars. Westminster Abbey has always had a greater High Church tendency since it is associated with medieval pageantry and the rituals of the monarchy, and this bias is revealed by the presence of the pyxes within the modern church, a feature that is lacking from many ordinary Anglican parishes.

Chapter House

---

25 "Visiting the Abbey: The Pyx Chamber" at the *Westminster Abbey Homepage*. Accessed online at: http://www.westminster-abbey.org/visit-us/highlights/the-pyx-chamber

The Chapter House

If the High Altar is the spiritual heart of Westminster, the Chapter House is its political focal point, and Westminster has always been at the center of English and British political life. The Chapter House is located in the old monk's cloister complex and is a room set off from the main area of the cloister by a hallway. This round open chamber was once the meeting room for the monks of Westminster, the place where the Abbot addressed his fellows, the spot where new abbots were chosen, and the site where the most important spiritual and political decisions were made. After the suppression of the monks, the building was renamed for the "Chapter," the assembly of the Dean of Westminster and the prebendaries for their regular meetings, along with other important groups like the King's Great Council and the early House of Commons. The room could be compared to a board room of a major corporation or charity, and it's fair to say the modern Chapter controls a large endowment and a number of employees and institutions. In fact, the Chapter now meets in a modern board room, and this room is open to the general public[26].

Poets' Corner

Picture of Poets' Corner

After leaving the relatively small spaces of the cloister, even the Chapter House seems small in comparison to the vastness of the sanctuary. Visitors can reenter the Abbey church from the south end of the transept and get an excellent side view ahead of the sacarum and the Shrine of St. Edward the Confessor. However, tour guides always ask visitors to head right to the southeastern corner of the transept, the location of a famous area called Poets' Corner. The administration of the Abbey has attempted over the centuries to invite England's most prestigious writers to have Westminster be the site of their burials, and while many have turned the invitation down, this is still perhaps the most impressive collection of literary figures in the English-speaking world.

The first literary burial to take place here was for Geoffrey Chaucer (1343-1400), the great

26 "Visiting the Abbey: The Chapter House" at the *Westminster Abbey Homepage*. Accessed online at: http://www.westminster-abbey.org/visit-us/highlights/the-chapter-house

royal poet who is considered by many to be the first great master of the English language. His masterpiece, *Canterbury Tales*, is still read to this day, even though the language has evolved so much over the centuries that it must often be read in translation into modern English. When Chaucer was interred here, the vicinity was not considered to belong to poets, but it was a desire of later generations to be buried close to the great master, akin to the way that later monarchs desired to be buried close to the venerated remains of St. Edward. The most well-known of those in Poets' corner include Ben Jonson (1572-1637), the playwright and contemporary of Shakespeare who was buried upright, the 17th century Poet Laureate John Dryden, and 19th century poet Robert Browning. Today, the tradition continues of memorializing (though not burying as space no longer permits) major writers and artists, such as C.S. Lewis and the founders of the Royal Ballet.

Sacarum and the Shrine of St. Edward the Confessor

The name "sacarum" is derived from Latin and roughly translates to "sacred place." This is the location of the High Altar, the focal point of every one of the great rituals performed in the Abbey since its foundation some 1,400 years ago. Like the Quire, the Sacarum has the feel of being a separate room; it has high walls but no ceiling, and it is divided from the main part of the nave by both stairs and decorative metal gratings. Visitors may ascend the steps into the Sacarum, but it's important to remember that the areas directly around the High Altar (called the "chancel") are only available for priests to walk on.

The great attraction here is not the Altar itself but the tomb located alongside it: the last resting place of King Edward the Confessor. Edward's place of pride is due to his unique historical status as England's only canonized monarch, not to mention the fact he was responsible for the construction of the first major church and palace at Westminster. Edward is still recognized as a saint among both the Anglicans and Catholics since his canonization occurred before the splintering of those faiths.

Henry VII's Lady Chapel

Behind (to the east of) and around the Sacarum is the Lady Chapel, rebuilt during the reign of King Henry VII (1457–1509), the first monarch of the Tudor dynasty. The last area of the Abbey Church to be built, it was created in a late Gothic Period style called the "Perpendicular Gothic."

The Chapel was dedicated to the Virgin Mary (the "Lady") and is famous for its remarkably beautiful fan ceiling. A fan ceiling is a form of structure where the room's supporting pillars split at their crowns like trees with multiple branches. These branches then fan out across the room, eventually meeting up with and merging into the branches of other altars. This gives a classic "ribbed" look to the ceiling. The Lady Chapel of Westminster is one of the finest examples of the style.

Within the Lady Chapel and the surrounding side chapels are buried an impressive number of monarchs. Desiring to be buried close to St. Edward, their holy ancestor, they cluster here behind the High Altar, primarily in raised stone tombs. The names here are often well-known: William III, Charles II, Henry VII, and the infamous half-sisters Mary, Queen of Scots and Elizabeth I, whose bloody rivalry - much of it relating to religious differences over Protestantism and Catholicism - almost led the kingdom into civil war in the 16th century. The viciousness of their mutual opposition is belied by the locations of their tombs, as the two queens lie close to each other in the Lady Chapel. Almost every English monarch was buried here until George II, who died in 1760. After George II, all subsequent monarchs were buried in Windsor Castle, if only because there simply wasn't enough room at Westminster.

One notable side chapel is the Royal Air Force (RAF) Chapel, which includes stained glass depictions of the Battle of Britain in 1940. Naturally, it commemorates the RAF's defense of the homeland against the German Luftwaffe and prevented a potential ground invasion of the British Isles.[27]

Perhaps the most infamous burial in the Lady Chapel was Oliver Cromwell, who headed the revolutionary government of the Commonwealth as the Lord Protector from 1653-1658. The only non-royal head of state in British history, he was given a full state burial after his death in the Chapel, but when the monarchy returned to power in 1660, his body was exhumed and posthumously executed[28].

---

27 "The Lady Chapel" at the homepage of *Westminster Abbey* accessed online at: http://www.westminster-abbey.org/visit-us/highlights/the-lady-chapel
28 "History: Oliver Cromwell and Family" at the homepage of *Westminster Abbey* accessed online at: http://www.westminster-abbey.org/visit-us/highlights/the-lady-chapel

A portrait of Cromwell

Transept and the Great North Door

Just within the Great North Door is a memorial to the United Kingdom's fallen military servicemen and women, a stone set in the floor that is usually surrounded by poppies (a symbol of bloodshed in battle in Britain and the British Commonwealth). This is only one of two prominent Tombs of the Unknown Warrior in London, the other being the Cenotaph in the old City of London where the yearly commemoration of Armistice Day occurs. While that larger monument takes place of pride in major ceremonies, its location in the center of a busy street makes it less accessible than this one in Westminster, which is an understandably popular stop for visitors to the Abbey.

Visitors with enough time can also find a number of other prominent non-Royal burials at Westminster. David Livingstone, the famed African explorer whose disappearance in 1865 led to a continent-spanning search by the American journalist Henry Stanley in 1871, was buried in the Abbey. Considered to be one of the greatest Britons of his day, after his death he was offered a space of honor in the Abbey near the Nave. While his heart was buried under a mpundu tree in today's Zambia, his embalmed body was carried by his attendants to the coast and was shipped to London[29].

Dr. Livingstone

St. Margaret's Church and the Surrounding Grounds

Alongside the great bulk of Westminster Abbey is a small stone building that is reminiscent of an English country church, and it is often completely overlooked by visitors. For worshipers seeking spiritual solace or students of the history of the British Parliament, however, there are few places that compare to the tranquil interior of St. Margaret's Church.

St. Margaret's was built in the same late Gothic style as Henry VII's Lady Chapel in the Abbey and was given over in 1614 to be the parish church of the Parliament's lower house, the House of Commons. The relatively lowly construction of the church of St. Margaret's in comparison to its

29 "History: David Livingstone" at the homepage of *Westminster Abbey* accessed online at: http://www.westminster-abbey.org/our-history/people/david-livingstone

neighbor is evidence of the formerly overwhelming power of the monarchy in British politics. The fact that the House of Commons is now the dominant institution of government is put into stark context when St. Margaret's indicates how far that body has risen over the last four centuries[30].

St. Margaret's

30 "St. Margaret's Church" at the homepage of *Westminster Abbey* accessed online at: http://www.westminster-abbey.org/st-margarets

Another important structure located on the grounds of the Abbey is the Westminster School, a world-renowned private Church of England (Anglican) school dedicated to educating the British elite. The construction of private schools like this is common throughout the Anglican Communion, and similar institutions can be found attached to cathedrals and even parish churches throughout Britain[31].

Another school associated with the Abbey is the Choir School, which trains and educates the boys to sing in the choir for the Abbey. An ancient Anglican tradition, that choir attends all religious services at the Abbey - from coronations to nightly Evensong - providing a beautiful and uniquely Anglican sound to the ancient halls[32].

Westminster Abbey continues to serve as the personal chapel of the House of Windsor, but it can safely be said that its everyday role is to serve as one of Britain's most important tourist destinations. Visitors who are not attending a religious ceremony such as Mass or Evensong are required to purchase an entry ticket near the Great West Door, in an alcove of the entrance that also has a small gift shop. Audio guides in various languages can be rented at the same time, or visitors can join in regular guided tours. During the open hours, the Abbey swarms with visitors, but this should not be viewed too harshly since the Abbey was a structure designed for precisely that purpose. If anything, it would be strange to see the Abbey empty of worshipers and visitors.

Tourism means the Abbey is a major moneymaker for the Church of England (with over a million visitors annually), and it also theoretically serves as a form of Christian evangelism for the masses. Like the medieval pilgrims, many modern visitors come to commune with the dead, though they are more likely to be delighted by Sir Isaac Newton than St. Edward the Confessor, and they will likely be more intrigued by Elizabeth I than the pious Henry VII.

Regardless, the Abbey's status as a premiere historical and religious site has been recognized by a number of bodies. It was given the United Kingdom's highest level of historical protection, "Grade I" listing on the Statutory List of Buildings of Special Architectural or Historic Interest, in 1958. An even greater honor was bestowed in 1987 when it was added to the United Nations Educations, Cultural and Scientific Organization's (UNESCO) list of World Heritage Sites, a tally of the most important sites in world history.[33]

The Tower of London

Origins of the Tower

The story of the Tower of London begins in 1066, when the Duke of Normandy, William,

---

31 Westminster School Homepage. Accessed online at: http://www.westminster.org.uk/
32 "Choir School" at the homepage of *Westminster Abbey* accessed online at: http://www.westminster-abbey.org/choir-school
33 "Palace of Westminster and Westminster Abbey including Saint Margaret's Church" at the *UNESCO World Heritage Site List*. Accessed online at: http://whc.unesco.org/en/list/426

landed at Pevensy in the south and marched to Hastings, where he defeated his rival, the Saxon king Harold, ending seven centuries of rule by the Germanic Saxon royal families. Looking back historically, this victory on the field of battle clinched the Norman Conquest, but it was not so obvious to those on the ground at the time. In fact, the Saxon elite chose a new king, Edgar, who rallied Saxon resistance, requiring William to march up the Thames until he reached the city of Southwark, which faced London across the river. Here, the Saxons actually won a victory, defending the London Bridge and the city itself. Knowing that London was the key to the kingdom, William marched east to a crossing and then headed back towards the capital. Edgar had been unable to raise a sufficient army to drive out the Normans, so when William arrived at the city gates, London surrendered and William was crowned in Westminster Abbey. William consolidated his rule and then returned to Normandy, henceforth known to history as William the Conqueror[34].

William and his half-brothers depicted in the Bayeux Tapestry

William the Conqueror is remembered for being the last foreign invader to conquer the island, but even then, the picture was not so simple, because the Saxons deeply resented Norman control and began rebellions in 1067, 1069, 1071 and 1075. Moreover, Harold's sons took control of Dublin and launched raids along the west coast of England for many years. The Normans gradually consolidated their control over the new kingdom primarily through the construction of a series of elaborate, expensive fortifications. These castles did have the purpose of protecting

---

34 "Essential Norman Conquest" by Osprey Publishing. Accessed online at:
   http://www.essentialnormanconquest.com/

England from outside assault (such as from the always troublesome Danes or the sons of Harold), but they were far more important for their ability to serve as points of control for dominating the English landscape and people, and the single most important fortification constructed during this period was the Tower of London, undoubtedly inspired by William's insights into the importance of that city for his campaign of 1066.

William's original tower was built for supremely practical reasons, as it represented the Normans' attempt to control the city of London. London has long served as the commercial hub of England, in large part because of the existence of the London Bridge, the only crossing of the River Thames for the majority of its length, and the Tower was positioned downriver from the Bridge, just within the Roman fortifications of the city[35]. Before the construction of the great ports of East London, all river traffic (and hence all traffic from the sea) had to pass up past the Tower into the Upper Pool where it was unloaded into the city. As a result, the Tower could benefit from (and strengthen) the existing fortifications of the city, control the routes of trade and potential invasion of the city by foreign powers, and serve as a social control over the city residents themselves.

Rafa Esteve's picture of the Tower of London and its position on the Thames

The relationship between the City of London and the Crown has been a complex one for now close to a thousand years, and when William arrived in London, he found a form of governance that was rooted in the time of the Roman Empire. Across the Empire, as the Romans colonized,

---

35 "London Bridge" in The Encyclopedia Britannica. Accessed online at:
   http://www.britannica.com/EBchecked/topic/347007/London-Bridge

they formed semi-autonomous local municipal governments based upon the Ancient Greek model, but when the Empire collapsed, these cities gained some semblance of independence. Though most of those in the Western Empire fell in the subsequent years, London retained its own government, which had not been created but instead simply recognized by the Saxon Kings[36].

William continued this relationship by "recognizing" the City with a charter, thereby giving his blessing to an institution that he did not control. To this day, the City of London (which is a single square mile around the financial district and St. Paul's Cathedral) is a unique administrative unit within the United Kingdom, where the laws of the UK (especially in regards to financial matters) do not completely apply. Today, this is primarily a mechanism by which "City" bankers subvert attempts to regulate their industry, but in the medieval period, this was a powerful check on royal authority in the region and a necessary evil for the Normans, who relied upon the City's economic weight to bolster their rule[37].

However they might have needed the City, William and his heirs did not fully trust it, and the creation of the Tower of London is only the most obvious marker of their desire to assert royal authority over the troublesome City and make sure that it primarily served royal needs, not its own. Of course, this control was never complete, but the subsequent history of the Tower is closely tied to the history of the city as it slowly rose to become a massive metropolis and the center of a global empire.

---

36 "London" in The Encyclopedia Britannica. Accessed online at:
http://www.britannica.com/EBchecked/topic/346821/London
37 "The Tax Haven in the Heart of Britain" by Nicholas Shaxson in *New Statesman* 24 February 2011

Bernard Gagnon's picture of the White Tower, the original structure

The Tower was not unique in this role as a multi-faceted expression of control. As archaeologist Matthew Johnson pointed out in his study of Bodiam Castle along the southeast coast of England, castles were traditionally seen as part of a wider national attempt to defend England from potential foreign invaders mimicking the Norman Conquest of 1066. Thus, Bodiam Castle was located along the River Rother, at the point where it was no longer easily navigable, making it the furthest spot upriver where an invasion fleet could disembark. Johnson's analysis has shown, however, that the Castle had more than this national defense role, as it was also designed to control a chokepoint in the movement of people and goods across the landscape. This checkpoint was an easy ford of the river, where food and wool and other goods crossed the water. In this way, the lord of the castle was able to exert political and economic control over the countryside without necessarily having to have his agents in every village and hearth of the hills[38].

---

38 "Understanding Bodiam: Landscapes Of Work At A Late Medieval English Castle" talk by Matthew Johnson given at Syracuse University. March 6th, 2014, 4pm.

The difference is that Bodiam Castle was a relatively small fortification located in a relatively marginal area of Britain, and its owner was a minor member of the nobility. The Tower, on the other hand, was a massive, carefully constructed military center which dominated the most important city and the most important river on the isle of Britain. Through the control over trade in London – on the Thames and on the London Bridge – the monarchy was able to assert its power over the economic life of the entire nation. While the Tower does not physically do this today since the shipping no longer passes beneath its crenellations, symbolically it still serves this role, asserting the ultimate authority of the British Monarchy and hence the State over the myriad financial transactions of the City of London's firms and their global reach. Of course, just like in the days of William, this control was never perfect or complete.[39]

The original Norman castle is today known as the White Tower. The current structure - expanded several times since - is constructed of stone and replaced the first fortification here: a timber fort raised up quickly after the Conquest. Work probably began in the late 1070s, and it was definitely done by the 1100s. The construction was a massive undertaking for the time, and the *Anglo-Saxon Chronicle* notes that "many shires whose labour was due to London were hard pressed because of the wall that they built around the Tower". The final building was easily the most impressive fortification in Britain: a square 36 meters by 32.5 meters and 27.5 meters tall at its greatest point. It was integrated into the Roman walls of the city (and was the first truly great piece of military architecture in Britain since their time), and it was further guarded by its own system of moats and dikes.[40]

39 "Tower of London" in the *Encyclopedia Britannica*. Accessed online at: Tower of London (tower, London, United Kingdom)
40 "Norman Beginnings" in the *Historic Royal Palaces: Tower of London* website. Accessed online at: http://www.hrp.org.uk/TowerOfLondon/sightsandstories/buildinghistory/normanbeginnings#sthash.HHnaqozK.dpuf

A medieval illustration of the White Tower

Michael Wal's picture of a suit of armor used by King Henry VIII now displayed in the White Tower

For William and his immediate descendants, the White Tower served a number of practical purposes. In addition to the defense of London from outside attack and control over the flows of goods, people and money through the City and its environs, the Tower was also home to numerous elements of the royal bureaucracy. It was, of course, home to the king during his time in the City, though it never rivaled the importance or opulence of the Palace of Westminster several miles upriver. Famously, it was also the only regular royal prison, and as such it housed numerous prisoners, famous and forgotten over the centuries. It was also at different times the location of the royal armory, treasury and even menagerie for the royal court.

While the White Tower was remarkable for its size and must have been awe-inspiring for the population of London and travelers at the time, including pilgrims and merchants passing through London, it was not particularly remarkable for its design. When the Normans arrived in Britain, they brought with them a relatively sophisticated understanding of military engineering and a well-established plan for the creation of their strongholds. The White Tower is just one of many similar structures, now fittingly called "Norman Keeps", that dotted the post-Invasion British landscape. Similar buildings can still be found in Rochester, Newcastle, Dover, Brough, Norwich, Guilford, Appleby, Castle Rising, Colchester and elsewhere.

The typical Norman Keep was a square structure, much taller than it was wide, with square towers rising above the main structures and protruding outwards from the main wall at each corner. Unlike the stereotypical castle of public memory, these keeps often did not have curtain walls (outer walls enclosing a courtyard), though the White Tower did, but stood alone on the landscape. The Keep served as living quarters for the noble owner, as well as a banquet hall, storage, living quarters for soldiers and servants, storage, and a chapel for the inhabitants.[41]

Panorama of the curtain walls

41 "Norman Square Keeps" accessed online at TimeRef. Available at: TimeRef - Medieval and Middle Ages History Timelines - Episodes of Medieval History

Bernard Gagnon's picture of St. John's Chapel inside the White Tower

In many ways, the White Tower is prototypical of this design, as it was built upon an ideal location, the flat lands around the Thames Valley, so its builders did not need to make any accommodations for topography. In addition to its size, the other major difference of the White Tower from the traditional design was a round tower on the northeast corner and an enlarged rounded-edge tower on the southeast corner. The building's designer was Gundulf of Rochester, a monk who crossed the Channel soon after the Norman invasion and was eventually appointed in 1075 as the Bishop of Rochester. Known as a military engineer, he would eventually supervise the construction of not only the White Tower but similar strongholds in Rochester and Colchester. Rochester Castle in particular takes the classic Norman Keep form and was built to control both the road from Rochester to London and the crossing of the River Medway (much as the White Tower controls the crossing of the Thames). Today, Gundulf is still known as the "Father of the Corps of Royal Engineers."[42]

---

42 "Rochester Castle" at the webpage of English Heritage, accessed online at: http://www.english-heritage.org.uk/daysout/properties/rochester-castle/

Norman Stronghold until the Anarchy

After the Norman Conquest, England and the Tower enjoyed only two generations of relative peace under the Norman Dynasty of William's heirs. The Tower was completed in 1079, and when William died in 1087 and was succeeded by his son, William Rufus, repairs were made for storm damage at the tower in 1091. The city during this period was mostly contained within the 326 acres enclosed by the Roman walls and home to between 30,000 and 40,000 inhabitants. It was a bustling place at the confluence of all of the major (Roman era) roads of the island, where influences, people and goods from across Britain and beyond converged. The homes were almost entirely made of wood and were only a few stories at most, making the great stone tower the most impressive structure in the City.[43]

The Norman overlords had consolidated their power during William's reign and ruled over a relatively peaceful and prosperous island. The first was William Rufus, who reigned from 1087 until 1100, and then his younger brother Henry I from 1100 to 1135 after William Rufus died in a hunting accident. After Henry's son and heir William died in the sinking of his ship, *The White Ship*, in 1120, the succession was put into doubt. His death from sickness in 1135 led to a crisis of succession and, then, into a bloody civil war. This war is known in history as "The Anarchy" and was fought between Stephen of Blois and the Empress Matilda. Stephen was the grandson of William the Conqueror through his mother, while Matilda was the daughter of Henry I. The Anarchy raged until 1154 and was not simply a war between two royal factions but a complete breakdown of law and order throughout England.

43 Hibbert 1971 21-23

A medieval illustration depicting Empress Matilda

Meanwhile, superb Norman military engineering in fortifications like the Tower of London had greatly outstripped the technology of siege engines, meaning that each side was able to hold onto its strongholds for extended periods and the enemy had to resort to prolonged sieges. Most of the war thus consisted of roving warrior bands associated with one faction or the other leaving their places of strength and ravaging the countryside around enemy strongholds, with the hope of depriving them of needed supplies. This, of course, was devastating for the countryside.

At times, the Tower seemed the only shelter in a storm of violence and danger. For most of the war, Stephen controlled London and the Tower – at first with support of the mob of London (a force of great power within the national politics), but at a later period in the war, he lost that support and was forced to retreat into the Tower while the citizenry besieged it[44]. In 1141, Matilda's forces temporarily defeated Stephen, and the Constable of the Tower - Geoffrey de Mandeville II - surrendered the stronghold to Matilda in return for forgiving the harsh fines imposed upon his father, the first Constable, for allowing Bishop Flambard to escape in 1101. Matilda arrived in the Tower, but when she attempted to have a coronation, the London mob drove her back and forced her to take refuge in the Tower. Eventually, she lost control of it again, and from that point forward she slowly lost the war.

This period also begins the tradition of using the Tower as a prison. The first prisoner held within its walls was Bishop Ranulf Flambard, who had served as the chief tax collector for King William Rufus. The taxes had been considered exorbitant, and the new king, Henry I, accused Ranulf Flambard of corruption and had him imprisoned in 1101. This was hardly a difficult sentence, however, since he had been in the Tower for barely six months before he staged a brazen escape. He threw a banquet (this was the extent of his freedom within the Tower) and got his guards drunk, and then escaped through a window in a rope smuggled in a wine jug. His allies were waiting at the foot of the Tower, and they escaped into the night. He would eventually ally with Henry's older brother, the Duke of Normandy, and aid him in a failed invasion of England before retiring from public life[45].

In many ways Bishop Flambard's time in the Tower was typical of the age. He was a powerful prisoner whose "crimes" consisted primarily of joining the wrong side in a political duel, but he remained influential enough to avoid execution. These individuals led lives of relative splendor in the Tower and still enjoyed most of the benefits of their rank.

However, there was a darker side to imprisonment that would emerge after Flambard's time: torture and execution. Today, the Tower's tortures and executions – and resulting tales of ghosts – are a source of both repulsion and grisly fascination for visitors and scholars alike. That said, to understand this role of the Tower, it's necessary to understand the mentality of the medieval torturer and executioner. French theorist Michel Foucault has written extensively on this topic, and he noted, "One no longer touched the body [in modern punishments], or at least as little as possible, and then only to reach something other than the body…" Thus, the torture was "an instrument, an intermediary" through which the punishing government attempted to manipulate the freedom, the spirit or the soul of the incarcerated. At the same time, this process was removed from the realm of public spectacle, which so often accompanied medieval torture[46]. Later, Foucault notes that the tortures of the Tower and elsewhere in Europe were "not an extreme expression of lawless rage" but instead a calculated application of a studied pain which is designed to carefully crescendo to the moment when the body ceases to live but can (and

---

44 Hibbert 30
45 "Ranulf Flambard" in the *Historic Royal Palaces: Tower of London* website. Accessed online at:
     http://www.hrp.org.uk/learninganddiscovery/Discoverthehistoricroyalpalaces/Prisoners/RanulfFlambard
46 *Discipline and Punish: Birth of the Prison* by Michel Foucault (1995). Pg 11

frequently did) continue long after physical death.

A torture device on display in the Tower

The public nature of the death was part of the process: "the fact that the guilty man should moan and cry out under the blows is not a shameful side-effect, it is the very ceremonial of justice being expressed in all its force... justice pursues the body beyond all possible pain." This was not for the purpose of reforming the offender but instead forcibly removing the stain of the crime upon the community of the state through the application of excessive violence[47].

---

47 *Ibid* pgs 33 - 34

This context, where royal rule was reinforced and reinstated after insurrection or crime through the complete annihilation of the offender, is crucial for understanding the Tower. Within the Tower, this type of torture and punishment did occur, but most frequently, these punishments occurred elsewhere, specifically the prison of Newgate and the gallows on Tyburn Hill. Instead, the Tower was the site of a different form of punishment from the norm. Most of the Tower executions occurred in "private" (within the courtyard and not in public spectacle) and were of the swift and – for the time – humane method of a single blow by a blade from the executioner without torture.

In fact, the executions in the Tower were not just abnormal but quite rare; only 22 people have been put to death in the Tower, compared to thousands at Tyburn. This is because they were not public spectacles or rituals of royal power, but instead tended to be more secretive events meant to eliminate political rivals or troublesome wives (in the case of Henry VIII) whose more open execution could be events for public outcry. These "private" executions were also considered to be more respectful and appropriate for those who the monarch felt should maintain some sense of decency.

Chris Nyborg's photo of the site of the scaffold

The Tower During the Plantagenet Dynasty

Peace returned to England in the summer of 1153 when the son of Matilda, Henry, signed a treaty with Stephen and was recognized as Stephen's heir. When Stephen died the following year, Henry II was crowned and the process of rebuilding began. Work began on the Tower in 1155, when Thomas Becket, at that point Archdeacon of Canterbury, Lord Chancellor of the Realm, was also made Keeper of the Works at the Tower. Becket would eventually be appointed Archbishop of Canterbury and would then be martyred on the grounds of Canterbury Cathedral by the King's men when he refused to accede to the Constitutions of Clarendon, a law which put the Church under the crown. Today he is recognized as St. Thomas Becket for his sacrifice and holiness.

A medieval depiction of Henry II and Thomas Becket

The Tower entered a quiet period after these repairs until the reign of Richard I, "the Lionheart" (1189 -1199). The son of Henry II, Richard began a project of impressive expansion before leaving to fight the Third Crusade in 1190. Richard left the Tower and England under the hands of his Lord Chancellor William Longchamp, the Bishop of Ely. Longchamp, realizing the precariousness of his position without his patron, quickly finished the Tower expansions. As knights refused to recognized Longchamp and turned to support Richard's brother, John, Longchamp attempted to besiege their castles, sparking a small-scale civil war that ended up with Longchamp besieged within the Tower of London. Eventually, the Tower fell to John, and though Longchamp escaped, John took the throne and held it until Richard's return.48

---

48 "The Medieval Tower" in the *Historic Royal Palaces: Tower of London* website. Accessed online at: http://www.hrp.org.uk/TowerOfLondon/sightsandstories/buildinghistory/medievalTower

The funeral effigy of Richard the Lionheart

After Richard's return, he eventually named John his successor. John I took the throne in 1199 and was frequently a guest at the Tower. In fact, it is believed that he was the first king to bring exotic animals, including lions, to live at the Tower, but in 1215, at the start of the next civil war (the First Barons' War), John's opponents seized the Tower as one of their first acts. The king died in 1216, and his nine-year old son, Henry III took the throne, eventually defeating the Barons.

Henry III was a remarkably long-lived and long-reigning king, holding the throne from 1216 until 1272, but the king's supporters - fearful of more revolt - realized the weaknesses in the Tower's defenses and in the 1220s expanded the fortress, adding the Wakefield and Lanthorn towers along the riverfront, ostensibly as lodging for the king and queen respectively. In 1238, there was another smaller uprising of the Barons, and the king fled to the Tower, during which he observed weaknesses in its defenses and began yet another building project. The king had massive walls, a watery moat and nine additional towers added on all of the Tower's landward sides. This was a time of uncertainty and fear and many London residents, seeing the ever-expanding Tower as a symbol of royal oppression, rejoiced when part of the walls and a tower near the Beauchamp Tower collapsed. Some attributed the event to the people's patron against royal excesses: St. Thomas Becket[49].

---

49 *Ibid*

A panorama with Wakefield Tower to the left and the White Tower to the right

Dirk Ingo Franke's picture of the former location of the moat

An amusing side note from this period was the 1251 arrival of a polar bear in the Tower. The walls of the fortress had become home to the royal menagerie, a proto-zoo for the enjoyment and prestige of the court, and since these bears had to be imported from the Norse colony of Greenland, they served as "spectacular status symbols" in the royal courts of Europe. The Norse hunters had to capture the bear alive without tranquilizers or firearms, tie it up, and bring it for weeks on their tiny boats down first to their settlements and then over the high seas to Europe. Given those difficulties, the presence of such a creature at the Tower of London demonstrated the immense prestige given to this particular fortification in the eyes of the monarchy[50].

In 1263, all of the tensions and fears broke out into the Second Barons' War which lasted until 1267. The baron Simon de Montfort rallied dissatisfied barons against the king and in 1263 rapidly captured much of southeast England. Henry and his son Edward I ("Longshanks") retreated to the Tower but were besieged their and eventually surrendered and were captured by Simon. In 1265, Edward escaped and rallied the royalists to his side, slowly beating back Simon and recapturing the Tower.

Bernard Gagnon's picture of a replica of Edward I's bedchambers in the Tower

Like his father, when Edward I came to power, he also went on a campaign of expanding the

50 *Collapse: How Societies Choose to Fail or Succeed* by Jared Diamond (2005). Viking Books. Pgs 240 - 243

Tower's defenses, recognizing its crucial role in any uprising. Thus, between 1275 and 1279, he turned his attention to the river-side defenses, and St. Thomas' Tower and the Traitor's Gate (a water gate where boats can enter the fortress) were created. Also during this period (1279 specifically) there is the first mention of the cost of buildings to house the Royal Mint within the Tower[51]. Edward also began the tradition of housing royal valuables in the Tower, creating a branch of the Royal Mint there and keeping much of his treasure safely out of the hands of his enemies and in its vaults.

A model of the expansion of the Tower conducted under Edward I

His son, Edward II (who ruled from 1307-1327), retreated to the Tower and lived there more-or-less permanently in response to regular uprisings by barons unhappy with his reign, but Edward II's son reversed the weakness of his father's reign and waged war on Scotland and France. In 1360, the Tower became the home of John II ("The Good"), the king of France, who lived there in splendor during his imprisonment. Finally, in the reign of Richard II, the kingdom was convulsed by the Peasants Revolt and the Tower was stormed by the mob of London, which captured and executed Simon of Sudbury, the Archbishop of Canterbury, in 1381. After the end of the rebellion, there were further repairs and expansions, including the Tower Wharf, which was supervised by Geoffrey Chaucer, the Clerk of Works in 1389 (and later author of *The Canterbury Tales*). Parallel to these internal threats was the ongoing brutality of the Hundred

---

51 "Royal Mint Timeline" at the Homepage of the *Museum of the Royal Mint*. Accessed online at: http://www.royalmintmuseum.org.uk/history/timeline/index.html

Years War (1337 - 1453), which was fought primarily in today's France but in which the Tower was also considered to be a part of a larger system of national defense.

In essence, with the exception of the White Tower, the Tower of London came to take its modern form largely during the troubled reigns of Richard I, Henry III and Edward I. The sprawling stronghold was a product of the military technology and propaganda demands of the time and is as much a symbol of royal instability in the late 1100s and throughout the 1300s as it is of royal power in the era. This was a period when England was drawn into a wider arena of European royal politics; under the Saxons, the island had been at first completely aloof from the larger European events, but after 1066, it was integrated into a larger state that included substantial holdings in France. Hence, the Tower was part of a much larger network of fortifications throughout England, Wales, Ireland[52], and northern and western France, typical of the military style of the time and remarkable more for its size than uniqueness.

The Tudors

The Tudors would rule England and its other territories from 1485-1603, but their kingdom was very different from that of the Normans and previous dynasties. Since it included no French lands, the Tudors were almost entirely focused upon England and the British Isles. By losing their continental lands in the Hundred Years War, the rulers of England had in essence become "English" again, and in the process London became the administrative, economic and military center of the state. In conjunction with that, the great fortress of the Tower was no longer one (albeit large) part of a vast network of fortifications but instead the beating heart of royal military power.

While the Norman period involved numerous military upsets and periods of violence, the first prolonged civil war since the Anarchy occurred in 1455 and lasted until 1487. Known as the Wars of the Roses, it pit the House of York against the House of Lancaster, both of which traced their ancestry back to William the Conqueror, and as in previous wars, the Tower remained a point of central concern for both parties. The upper hand passed back and forth between the two, and in 1471, the Yorkists held the Tower and used it to first imprison and then execute Henry VI, the Lancastrian king and great-grandson of Richard II. In this act, the House of Lancaster was extinguished by the Yorkists, but their cause was taken up by the House of Tudor from Wales. During the War, the Tower served as a place of not only control but also celebration, most notably as a safe place to hold the coronation of Edward IV.

---

52 Dublin Castle, for example, was built after 1204 on the orders of John I - consolidating his family's conquest of 1169. It was probably the most far-flung of such castles.

Portrait of Henry VI

Richard Nevell's picture of the room in the Wakefield Tower where Henry VI died

During these conflicts, both sides imprisoned their enemies in the Tower when they held control of it, and perhaps the most famous prisoner of the era was Sir Thomas Malory, an apparent Yorkist rogue who was accused of ambushing the Lancastrian Duke of Buckingham and of seducing the wives of Lancastrian noblemen. While imprisoned in the tower before his death in 1471, he took the time to pen *Le Morte d'Arthur*, the first major compilation of the tales of King Arthur. It is likely that as a prisoner, he had access to an excellent library that he drew upon in the Tower, as well as the time and resources with which to write.

This was also the period of one of the most haunting stories of the Tower: the Princes in the Tower. The two boys, Edward and Richard, were the sons of the Yorkist King Edward IV (who had captured and executed Henry VI), and like previous kings, Edward IV had stored his most precious "treasures" in the Tower during times of danger, in this case his two sons and heirs. When the boys were 12 and 9, respectively, their father died, perhaps of typhoid fever but also possibly of poison. The King named his brother - Richard - the Lord Protector of the kingdom and guardian of his two sons. Soon after, young Edward - today considered Edward V despite never being crowned - and his brother disappeared from the public eye. Their uncle, Richard III, took the throne in 1483 and has been often accused by historians of killing the two, though there are several other suspects.

John Everett Millais' painting, "The Two Princes in the Tower"

Two years later, in 1485, Richard III fell on the field of battle at Bosworth while fighting against Henry Tudor, who became the king of the new dynasty, and some insisted that the loss of faith in his rule due to his apparent murder of his nephews weakened Richard's Yorkist side. Nonetheless, the princes' disappearance continued to haunt the Tudors for some time after, especially when a lad named Lambert Simnel was said to be the young prince Richard by a group of Yorkists in 1487. Under the basis of Simnel's legitimacy, they attempted to revolt against Henry Tudor, and from 1491-1497, another supposed Richard, a man named Perkin Warbeck, attacked the western territories, costing the Tudor state a considerable amount in wealth, attention and military power.

To prevent similar occurrences, Henry Tudor, who became Henry VII, took the throne in 1485 and married Elizabeth of York, the older sister of the two Princes. In this way, he claimed to have united both of the rival lines within his own dynasty and created a single, unified English national house. Nearly two centuries later, in 1674, the bodies of two youths were found in construction works at the Tower and were widely (though never conclusively) believed to be the Princes. Charles II had them buried in Westminster Abbey.

Paul Delaroche's "King Edward V and the Duke of York in the Tower of London"

It was during Henry VII's reign in 1485 that the King ordered the foundation of a new military unit specifically associated with the Tower: the Yeomen Warders (popularly called the "Beefeaters"). The Tudors were rulers of breathtaking ambition, letting no earthly power - not even the Pope or the lives of his wives in the case of Henry VIII - stand in the way of their goals. At the same time, they were also innovators of social, political and military policies that helped to forge the centralized English state. One of these many innovations was the creation of a new unit specifically created for guarding the royal houses: the Yeomen. Drawn from the population of freemen ("yeomen") without direct ties to other lesser nobles, the Tudor kings felt they could rely upon this particular unit to protect their own persons. In 1509, when Henry moved out of the Tower of London once peace had settled on the Kingdom, he left a token force of these Yeomen to protect the property, and in effect, he created two of the oldest units in the British military: the Yeomen Warders of the Tower of London and the Yeomen of the Guard, who continued to guard him in his new home. Today, they are the oldest units in the British military and the first permanent standing military force created outside of the system of feudal ties.[53]

53 "Yeoman Warders" in the *Historic Royal Palaces: Tower of London* website. Accessed online at: http://www.hrp.org.uk/TowerOfLondon/stories/yeomanwarder

The uniform of Yeomen Warders

There was a growing centralization of other elements of the state as well. One impact on the Tower was the final closure in 1540 of all of the coin mints in the hands of ecclesiastical authorities by Henry VIII, which left the Royal Mint in the Tower as the only source of coins in the realm[54].

However, the reign of the Tudors at the Tower is not primarily remembered for the creation of the Yeoman Warders but instead for its use as the prison for royal women of the era. Four famous women were held here: Anne Boleyn, Lady Jane Grey, Catherine Howard and Elizabeth Tudor (who would become Elizabeth I). All but Elizabeth were executed on the grounds, with Anne and Catherine killed on the orders of Henry VIII. Elizabeth, on the other hand, was not imprisoned until the reign of her sister Mary I, when she was imprisoned in 1554 at the height of

---

54 "Royal Mint Timeline" at the Homepage of the *Museum of the Royal Mint*. Accessed online at:
http://www.royalmintmuseum.org.uk/history/timeline/index.html

Wyatt's Rebellion. She was held first in the Tower and then under house arrest for a year until she was released shortly before her sister's death.

Portrait of Anne Boleyn

In addition to Elizabeth, Anne, Jane, and Catherine, Henry VIII also filled the Tower with an unprecedented number of other prisoners, most of whom were unrepentant Catholics. The most prominent of these was Sir Thomas More, the author of *Utopia*, who was imprisoned in the Tower in 1534 while he was Lord Chancellor. More was imprisoned due to his opposition to Protestantism and to the King's marriage to Anne Boleyn, until he was executed in 1535[55].

---

55 "The Tudors" in the *Historic Royal Palaces: Tower of London* website. Accessed online at:

Portrait of Sir Thomas More

Sir Thomas More's tomb at the Tower of London

The imprisonment of Elizabeth in particular reveals how confinement in the Tower was not always a symbol of royal omnipotence but actually the monarch's frequent impotence. Elizabeth was viewed as a threat to her sister, who sought to marry the Catholic King Phillip of Spain and was widely believed to desire to impose Catholicism upon the nation. Elizabeth was massively popular among the populace, which forced Bloody Mary to act. Mary felt she could not allow her sister the freedom to move about the kingdom after the events of Wyatt's Rebellion, and yet she also feared that killing her sister would spark a much wider rebellion. In her impotence, she took the only (ultimately ineffective) act she could by imprisoning Elizabeth within the Tower.

Bloody Mary

Since its creation, the Tower has sat at the heart of the great events of state. During the reign of Henry VIII (1509 -1547), affairs of the state came to be centered upon one great question: Catholicism or Protestantism. Henry declared England to be independent of the Church in Rome and dissolved all of the monasteries under his dominion. The repercussions of this event have echoed ever since, as it also created the Church of England (often called the "Anglican" or

"Episcopalian" Church). The conflict between Mary and Elizabeth - which in previous generations would have been purely dynastic in nature[56] - had a strongly religious air as well, since those who supported reunification with Rome sided with Mary and those who didn't supported Elizabeth, even as she was locked away in the Tower. With the ascension of Elizabeth, the Protestant faction was solidified in their position and the Arch-Catholic King Philip of Spain was denied his ability to convert England by marrying Mary. All throughout England, and the Tower of London was no exception, fortifications were bolstered and military resources were gathered in anticipation of the coming English invasion which finally occurred in the form of the 1588 Spanish Armada.

The Tower During the House of Stuart and the English Civil Wars

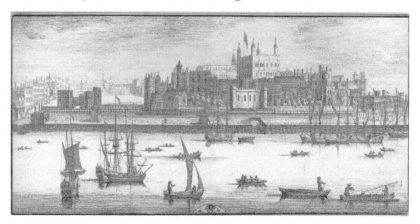

An 18th century engraving of the Tower of London

Elizabeth I was known as the "Virgin Queen" because she never took a husband nor bore children, so when she died, it was the end of the Tudor line of kings and queens. The Crown instead fell to the House of Stuart, which at that time had been the royal house of Scotland since 1371. As a result, Elizabeth was succeeded by King James I (King James VI of Scotland), the son of Mary, Queen of Scots, who had been briefly imprisoned by Elizabeth I in the Tower between 1569 and 1570 and executed by her in 1587.

James moved to London in 1603, arriving first at the Tower of London, and after his coronation he continued his predecessor's work of strengthening Protestantism in the kingdoms. Perhaps his best known work was when he ordered the translation of the Bible - fittingly named the King James Version - between 1604 and 1611. Naturally, James' continued support of the Church of England led to ongoing resistance during his reign, the most famous event of which

---

56 Like the conflicts between the Lancastrians and Yorkists or between Matilda and Stephen.

was the so-called "Gunpowder Plot" of 1605, when Guy Fawkes and his conspirators attempted to blow up Parliament and kill the King. When Fawkes was captured, he was held and tortured at the Tower before his execution.

Despite that execution, the Tower's history in the early 1600s do show that the monarchy under James I was not rigidly anti-Catholic but instead aimed to walk a fine line of diplomacy between its own Protestantism (and that of many of its subjects) and the powerful Catholic states of mainland Europe, especially Spain. Thus, when the famous Sir Walter Raleigh offended the Catholic King Philip III of Spain with his ceaseless raids on the coast of South America and his search for the golden city of El Dorado, James I bowed to Spanish outrage and had the privateer imprisoned in the Tower several times until his last stint in 1618, after which he was beheaded at Westminster Palace[57].

The tensions and pressures within the religious situation became further complicated when many Protestants began to view the monarchy as "backsliding" towards Catholicism. Some of this may have been inevitable, as the Protestantism that was taking hold among the growing merchant classes of the urban centers (the "Puritans") was strongly Calvinist and rejected ritual, finery and the demonstration of wealth, all of which were central to the early modern monarchy. However, the tension was exacerbated by the second monarch of the House of Stuart: Charles I (reigned from 1626-1649). Charles' falling out with the Puritans began when he attempted to marry a Spanish princess in 1623, and it worsened after his subsequent marriage to a Catholic French princess in 1625. He asserted his right to absolute divine rule and promoted those elements of the Church of England and the Church of Scotland[58] that desired to bring ritual more closely in line with the Catholic faith.

In London, Charles was concerned about the growing unrest throughout his dominions and appointed Colonel Thomas Lunsford Lieutenant of the Tower in 1641. Lunsford was infamous as a murderer and an outlaw yet was loyal to Charles (who had pardoned him) and was considered a vicious and effective commander. Public outcry led to his removal from office four days later, but he served as the commander of the Westminster guard after that and led his soldiers to slaughter protesting citizens of London several times[59]. These and other conflicts with Parliament finally led to the outbreak of the Wars of the Three Kingdoms, of which the English Civil Wars are the best known element.

The King held the Tower via the office of Lieutenant Conyers (who was loyal to him) at the beginning of the civil war, but the strength of the Parliamentarian and Puritan forces in London

---

57 For more or Sir Walter Raleigh's adventures in South America and his search for El Dorado, read *El Dorado: The Search for the Fabled City of Gold* by Jesse Harasta and the Charles River Editors (2014).
58 Two independent Protestant churches both under his nominal control - today often called the Anglican/Episcopalian (Church of England) and Presbyterian (Church of Scotland) churches.
59 "Sir Thomas Lunsford c. 1611-56" at the homepage of the *British Civil Wars, Commonwealth and Protectorate 1638-1660 Project*. Accessed online at: http://bcw-project.org/biography/sir-thomas-lunsford

led to the fall of the Tower in 1643, something they saw as a key element in their defense and control of London. Understanding the importance of the site, the Parliamentarian forces were the first to establish a permanent garrison in the Tower, something which has continued ever since[60]. Overall, the quick capture of the Tower deprived Charles' forces of a crucial strategic advantage and may have contributed significantly to his eventual fall. It also ensured that the Tower was not the site of a prolonged siege during the Civil Wars, and hence the structure suffered relatively little damage in the war as opposed to areas that did see battles, like Glouchester or Bristol. Oliver Cromwell and his New Model Army slowly consolidated control over the three kingdoms of England, Scotland and Ireland after Charles's capture in 1645, and he was executed in 1649.

Under the revolutionary government, the office of Lieutenant of the Tower (by this time the Lieutenants ran the day-to-day operations of the Tower while the Constable office was ceremonial) was retained but given to a radical Puritan and the current Lord Mayor, Isaac Penington, who had zealously attempted to remove what he considered idolatrous images from the churches of London. Penington served on the court that convicted Charles I, but after the restoration of the Monarchy in 1660, he was imprisoned until his death in 1661 in the very same Tower that he had ruled over[61].

During Cromwell's Commonwealth (1649-1661), there were some changes made to the Tower, most notably the fact that the Crown Jewels were removed and melted down and sold. However, in many ways, it remained central to the national administration as a prison for politically powerful enemies, a military stronghold for controlling and protecting London, and a central storehouse for distribution of military supplies throughout the realms. In particular, Cromwell used it to hold those members of the revolutionary movements who called for a reorganization of the social order and wealth to include not simply removing the king but a leveling of wealth (the "Levellers"). For instance, Leveller firebrand writer John Lilburne was held there in 1646 and 1647 in order to stop him from publishing his vitriolic attacks against the hypocrisies of Cromwell's government,[62] as well as his ally Edward Sexby, who rose up against Cromwell in 1653 to demand a more democratic form of government. Sexby was imprisoned in the Tower in 1656 and died of a fever in its walls in 1658[63].

Cromwell's ascension to the king-like status of "Lord Protector" in 1653 alienated many of his more radical followers, and even more turned away from the Commonwealth government after his death in 1658 and the appointment of his unpopular son Richard Cromwell to his position.

---

60 "History of the Tower of London" accessed online at: http://www.ancientfortresses.org/history-of-tower-of-london.htm
61 "Isaac Penington c. 1584 - 61" at the homepage of the *British Civil Wars, Commonwealth and Protectorate 1638-1660 Project*. Accessed online at: http://bcw-project.org/biography/isaac-penington
62 "John Lilburne c. 1615 - 57" at the homepage of the *British Civil Wars, Commonwealth and Protectorate 1638-1660 Project*. Accessed online at: http://bcw-project.org/biography/john-lilburne
63 "Edward Sexby c. 1616 - 58" at the homepage of the *British Civil Wars, Commonwealth and Protectorate 1638-1660 Project*. Accessed online at: http://bcw-project.org/biography/edward-sexby

That move smacked of monarchy, and in 1659, Richard fled into exile and was replaced by a Committee of Safety that dissolved Parliament after the surviving Rump Parliament and the Council of State attempted (and failed) to rule the country in 1659. Governance began to implode, and in 1660, Charles II (Charles I's son) declared himself king. Returning to England, he set up Sir John Robinson as first the Lieutenant and Constable of the Tower in 1660 (continuing until 1679) and then Lord Mayor of London in 1662.

Popular legend holds that the reign of Charles II also marked an important beginning for the folklore of the Tower: the arrival of the ravens. It is certainly possible that ravens had frequented the Tower before this point, as the birds are native to Britain and may have been attracted by the Tower's regular executions and their gruesome habit of eating the eyes of the dead. However, in the centuries after Charles' Restoration, the city grew up around the Tower, and the ravens were extirpated from the surrounding countryside, leaving the Tower's colony as the only remaining ravens among the previous population.

Over time, the legend grew that as long as ravens remained within the Tower, the kingdom - and the monarchy - would not fall, and by the 20th century, this story (which was popularized by the always romantic Victorians) had such appeal that Winston Churchill went about recruiting ravens to replace those killed in the bombs of the Blitz. Since World War II, the British government has recognized the ravens as being enlisted in the military, though some have even been "dismissed" from service after causing particular difficulty for keepers[64]. The Tower takes their birds seriously, and when avian flu threatened the population in 2006, special custom-built indoor aviaries were built on the Tower grounds to isolate them from the disease[65].

---

64 "Myths of the Raven: The Myths and Meanings of the Tower of London Ravens" by Jeffrey Vallance (2007) in *The Fortean Times*. Accessed online at:
http://www.forteantimes.com/features/articles/879/myths_of_the_raven.html
65 "Bird Flu Threat Sends Tower of London Ravens Indoors" by the Associated Press 21 Feb 2006 in *Fox News Online*. Accessed online at: http://www.foxnews.com/story/2006/02/21/bird-flu-threat-sends-tower-london-ravens-indoors/

Philippe Kurlapski's picture of one of the Tower's ravens

New threats emerged as the Stuarts reestablished themselves. Spain had been eclipsed as it was exhausted militarily and financially by the century-long, brutal Dutch Revolt (1568-1648), but the victors of those wars, the Dutch Republic, was entering its age of glory: the Dutch Golden Age. The English and Dutch became growing rivals during the late 1660s as each sought to become the premier mercantile power in their overseas empires, and fears of a potential Dutch invasion led the Stuart military to reinvest in the defenses of the Tower of London, including reinforcing its walls against cannonades[66].

66 "From Royalty to Artillery" by Robert Wilde. Accessed online at:
http://europeanhistory.about.com/od/ukandireland/a/prtol4.htm

The Tower was clearly in an era of transition at this point, even though the military roles that it had taken up during the wars and the Commonwealth period remained, including the permanent garrison, the storage of artillery, gunpowder and ammunition, and the administration of the distribution of military supplies throughout the Empire. At the same time, it began to take on some of the earlier, royal roles as well, serving as the home of the royal menagerie, the Yeoman Warders in their Tudor-era regalia, and the storage of royal treasures, especially the Crown Jewels. While the Royal Mint was kept within the Tower, it was completely modernized; in 1662, the new king had screw presses and rolling mills imported for the Mint, removing the hand-striking method that had been used since Roman times[67].

One of Charles II's first acts was to restore the Crown Jewels. While a few items remained intact, such as the Coronation Spoon and the Coronation Chair (which Cromwell sat in when he was invested as Lord Protector), the majority of the items had been broken apart and sold. Restoring the Crown Jewels was seen as necessary for a coronation, and the government spent the princely sum of £12,185 to recreate them[68].

67 "Royal Mint Timeline" at the Homepage of the *Museum of the Royal Mint*. Accessed online at: http://www.royalmintmuseum.org.uk/history/timeline/index.html
68 "The Crown Jewels" at the *Official Website of the British Monarchy*. Accessed online at: http://www.royal.gov.uk/MonarchUK/Symbols/TheCrownJewels.aspx

A replica of St. Edward's Crown

Soon after the Stuart Restoration, the brand new Crown Jewels were once again threatened by a ghost from the Cromwellian past: Colonel Thomas Blood. Born in Ireland in 1618, Blood was originally a soldier for the King in the Civil Wars but switched sides (like many did) when it was obvious that the Monarchy was going to fall. In return, he was made a Justice of Peace and given a large estate. Upon the restoration of Charles II, Blood and his family fled to his native Ireland where, with other deposed Cromwellians, he attempted to capture Dublin Castle and seize the Governor. When that failed, he fled to France, only to make his way back to England and try (again unsuccessfully) to capture the Governor of Ireland in 1670.

The frustrated schemer next turned his attention to the Crown Jewels. The plotter befriended the Keeper of the Jewels and proposed a marriage between his nephew and the Keeper's daughter. During the marriage negotiations, they asked to see the Jewels (already a popular tourist destination) and attacked the Keeper when he opened the door. They hid the Jewels on their persons by flattening the crown with a mallet and tried to shoot their way out of the Tower. They were captured, but, incredibly, they were subsequently pardoned by the King; in fact, Blood lived until 1680 and was a popular figure at Charles' court. He was the last man to steal the Crown Jewels.[69]

69 "The Theft of the Crown Jewels" by Ben Johnson. At *Historic UK: The History and Heritage Accommodation Guide*. Accessed online at: http://www.historic-uk.com/HistoryUK/HistoryofEngland/The-Theft-of-the-Crown-Jewels/

Thomas Blood

From Charles II onwards, the Stuarts continued their habit of leaning towards Catholicism and, particularly damning for the increasingly patriotic English, France. Charles II had stayed in France during Cromwell's Commonwealth, and his mother, Henrietta Maria[70], was French Catholic. After Charles's death, his younger brother James took the throne, but his reign was characterized by growing conflict with Parliament, especially over his desire to promote tolerance for Catholics and non-Anglican Protestants. James only ruled for four years (1685-1688), and the final straw was the birth of his son, James Francis Edwards (famed as "The Old Pretender," or to the Jacobites, "The King Over the Water"). Baby James was christened in his

---

70 For whom the colony (and eventual state) of Maryland - a haven for English Catholics - was named.

mother's faith, Roman Catholicism, and things came to a head when the two parties in Parliament (the Tories and Whigs) united and invited Mary - James II's Protestant elder daughter - and her Protestant husband, William of Orange of the Netherlands, to reign. William and Mary[71] arrived at the head of an invading army in what the English remember as "The Glorious Revolution" but which is more infamous in Ireland for its victory in the 1690 Battle of the Boyne. James fled to France and lived there as the "Jacobite" pretender to the throne for the rest of his natural life.

In England, the new royal family consolidated its Protestant control over the kingdom. In the Tower, James' loyal Constable George Legge was replaced by William's loyal man Robert Lucas, the Third Baron Lucas. After the death of William (he was preceded by Mary) in 1702, Mary's younger sister, Queen Anne, took the throne until 1714. She also replaced the Constable upon taking the throne - her favored Montagu Venables-Bertie was made Constable. Like her sister, she bore no children, so upon her death, the Parliament of the United Kingdom sought out her nearest non-Catholic heir: George I of the German House of Hanover.

The Tower and the British Empire

By the dawn of the 18th century, the Tower's role as a fortification had become largely outdated. The city had sprawled so massively around the Tower that it could no longer effectively defend it, especially the eastern dock regions that stretched far downriver from it. National defense was centered upon the Royal Navy, meaning an enemy that reached the Tower had already fought their way to the heart of the Empire. Likewise, the ability for the Tower to serve as a social control over London had declined alongside the growth of the City, eventually leading to the creation of the Metropolitan Police Force ("Scotland Yard") in 1829 in order to recreate a system of centralized, state-dominated control over the growing metropolis[72].

Thus, it was inevitable that over the course of the 18th and 19th centuries, the Tower was gradually decentralized from the role of administration and maintenance of law and order, and it started to become the more purely symbolic touristic attraction it is today. One element of this was the declining number of prisoners and executions on the site. The final beheading in English history was of Simon Fraser, the Lord Lovat, who was executed on April 9, 1747 after participating in the failed Jacobite Uprising of 1745. The Jacobites, who hailed among the Highland Clans of Scotland, unsuccessfully attempted to overthrow the House of Hanover and return the Stuarts to the throne[73].

That said, the Tower continued to be used for housing prisoners of particular political importance, such as Lord George Gordon, who was imprisoned in 1780 after instigating the

---

71 For whom the College of William and Mary in Virginia was named (they signed the original letters of patent in 1693).

72 "Timeline 1829-1849" at the homepage of the *Metropolitan Police Force*. Accessed online at: http://content.met.police.uk/Site/historicaltimeline

73 "Simon Fraser, Lord Lovat" accessed online at: http://iainthepict.blogspot.com/2011/04/simon-fraser-lord-lovat.html

"Gordon Riots," a massive pro-Catholic street protest. Alongside Gordon, the Tower in 1780 also held Henry Laurens, the former President of the rebellious Continental Congress of the American colonies; Laurens was the only American ever held at the Tower. 1780 was also the last year of hangings at the Tower; after this point, the non-public method of firing squad remained the only form of execution at the Tower.

Henry Laurens

The Tower served admirably in the Napoleonic Wars as the nerve center for the great effort to convert Britain's burgeoning industrial might into military power, with the Tower serving as the primary place where the British gathered war material from across the realm and sent it to battlefields across Europe. After the Wars, the great hero of Waterloo, Arthur Wellesley, the Duke of Wellington, was appointed the Constable of the Tower, by this time considered one of the most prestigious honors given to a member of the British armed forces[74]. Wellesley used his

74 From *The London Gazette* 13 February 1827. Issue 18335 Page 340. Accessed online at:

time as Constable to make some reforms, most notably transforming the Yeoman Warders from an active military unit into a reward for non-commissioned officers with 22 years of exemplary service[75].

The Duke of Wellington

While the development of artillery made the Tower's stone walls obsolete as a military defense (though obviously not obsolete as a prison), it remained a military base and was the headquarters of the Board of Ordnance until 1855. This was no minor role, because in the 19th century, the Board was the second largest government department in the United Kingdom after the Treasury and included a number of roles: manufacturer of gunpowder and armaments, the Royal Military

https://www.thegazette.co.uk/London/issue/18335/page/340
75 "Yeoman Warders" in the *Historic Royal Palaces: Tower of London* website. Accessed online at: http://www.hrp.org.uk/TowerOfLondon/stories/yeomanwarder

Academy, the Royal Engineers and Artillery, the maintenance of fortifications throughout the Empire, the Royal Observatory in Greenwich, the national mapmaking service (the "Ordnance Survey") and many other minor elements of national defense. While some cannons and small arms were stored in the White Tower in this period, the Tower of London was primarily an administrative center for the body. Its closure in 1855 was due to the Board's spectacular failure in provisioning the military in the Crimean War, leading to its dissolution and the incorporation of its elements into the War Office (and from there into the modern Ministry of Defense).

Alongside the Board, much of the crowded space within the Tower was taken up by the Mint. Plans drawn up in 1701 by William Alingham show that the Mint at that point took up all of the space between the inner and outer walls on the three sides not facing the river. The continued growth of the economic might of Great Britain, not to mention the coinage needs of its far-flung colonies, meant that it finally grew out of the limited space within the Tower. Thus, in 1804, work began on a steam-powered facility on nearby Tower Hill (close to where the public beheadings used to take place)[76]. The Tower Hill facility would completely replace the space in the Tower by 1809, where it remained, within sight of the Tower, until its final closure in 1980.

76 "Royal Mint Timeline" at the Homepage of the *Museum of the Royal Mint*. Accessed online at:
http://www.royalmintmuseum.org.uk/history/timeline/index.html

Bryan MacKinnon's picture of the scaffolding site for Tower Hill

In 1835, a further major change and a break from over six centuries of tradition occurred when the animals of the menagerie - with the sole exception of the rooks - were moved to the relatively new (1828) London Zoo in Regent's Park. The only animals that remained were the increasingly-famous ravens, whose care was given over to the new position of "Ravenmaster of the Yeoman Warders."

In 1876, the Tower's the Yeoman Warders, the famed "Beefeaters," were further brought into the consciousness of the world through the creation of Beefeater Gin by Burrough's distillery in London. The bottle, then and now, bore an image of the distinctive Beefeater in uniform, and its worldwide distribution has helped to make the Beefeaters famous and turn them into one of the most important attractions of the Tower.[77]

Alongside the administrative purposes, the Tower was increasingly becoming an important destination for visits to the City, particularly because of the presence of the Crown Jewels. The

---

77 "The World's Most Awarded Gin: History" at the *Beefeater Homepage.* Accessed online at: http://beefeatergin.com/awarded/history

tension between a desire to make these important symbols of the Monarchy available for public admiration and the need to protect them from theft remained. In 1815, a woman reached through the bars protecting the Jewels and attempted to pull the crown through the gap, badly damaging it. She was later found to be legally insane, but additional protections were created, most notably a prohibition on allowing people to touch the objects. The Jewels were further threatened in 1841 when the building next to the Jewel House caught fire. Since the key to the Jewels was inside this building, a police officer wrenched open the protective grate with a crowbar, and the Yeoman Warders were seen carrying the objects by hand through the crowds and into the White Tower[78].

The Tower's Recent History

The dawn of the 20th century saw more changes to the Tower and to England. The last ruler of the House of Hanover was Queen Victoria (her husband was of the German House Saxe-Coburg and Gotha), and her son, Edward VII, was considered to be the first of his line. The family was of German origin, but in the midst of the passionate anti-German sentiments during World War I, the family changed their name to the House of Windsor.

Under the Windsors, the Tower's role continued to shift. Already, the great administrative departments of the Royal Mint and the Board of Ordnance (not to mention the important but non-administrative Royal Menagerie) had been moved out of the Tower, and the tradition of public executions on Tower Hill had been suspended. Still, the Tower continued as a prison for the first half of the 20th century, and one prominent prisoner of this period was Roger Casement. A diplomat and member of the Foreign Service, Casement had been knighted and recognized for his work in the Belgian Congo and then the Peruvian Amazon, where he laid bare the brutalities and slavery in those countries' rubber industries. He became a public figure in this period, leading an international crusade against such abuses, but in his later years, Casement – an ardent anti-imperialist – joined the struggle for the independence of his native Ireland. He was arrested during the Easter Rebellion for attempting to raise Irish volunteers to fight on the side of Germany for Irish independence and was imprisoned in the Tower for much of 1916, when he was further embroiled in an ugly scandal over the revelations that he was gay. He was hung in Pentonville Prison on the 3rd of August, 1916, and to this day, his name is still remembered in Ireland, the Congo and Peru as a fighter for liberty[79].

---

78 "Visiting the Crown Jewels: A Brief History" at the in the *Historic Royal Palaces: Tower of London* website. Accessed online at: http://www.hrp.org.uk/CrownJewels/Abriefhistory

79 He became particularly well known after Peruvian author Mario Vargas Llosa published *El Sueno del Celta* (The Dream of the Celt) in 2010, a text that was crucial in his receiving the Nobel Prize for Literature that year.

Casement

Many of the later prisoners in the Tower were associated with the military, as it was revived as a military prison during World War II. Rudolf Hess, Adolf Hitler's Depute Fuhrer, was imprisoned there for four days in 1941 after making a secret flight to England to attempt to negotiate a peace treaty. Prominent German spy Josef Jakobs was also held in the Tower in 1941 and, after being found guilty of espionage, was executed at the Tower's practice firing range, which made him the last individual to be put to death at the Tower[80]. The last prisoners to be

---

80 "Josef Jakobs" at *British Military and Criminal History.* Accessed online at: http://www.stephen-stratford.co.uk/josef_jakobs.htm

held at the Tower were famed East London gangsters Reggie and Ronnie Kray, who had failed to turn up for their National Service (as conscripted soldiers); when their regiment was attached to the Tower, they were held there briefly in 1952[81].

Jakobs

The other remaining administrative role that the Tower continues to fill is the holding place for the Crown Jewels. This ostensibly protective role for the Tower fits well into its growing role as a tourist spot, given that the Jewels are one of the great attractions for the site, and they have only grown in fame over the 20th century as they have increased in value. For instance, in 1910, the Great Star of Africa (the "Cullinan Diamond") was added to the Scepter, and in 1911 the Imperial Crown of India was created to commemorate George V's (the son of Edward VII) visit to India[82].

This remnant of administrative duty aside, today the Tower is almost completely dedicated to serving as a tourist attraction in the heart of London. The Yeoman Warders have become colorfully-dressed tour guides, wearing their Tudor-era dress uniforms as their work costumes. The White Tower is a museum, and there are also displays of coins from the old Royal Mint and an exhibition dedicated to the Royal Menagerie.

Today, the Tower is administered under the Historic Royal Palaces organization, along with several other properties owned by the Queen "in right of Crown," including Hampton Court

81 "Great Misconceptions: Rudolf Hess was the last prisoner kept in the Tower of London" by Justin Pollard. Accessed online at: http://www.historyextra.com/blog/great-misconceptions-0

82 "The Crown Jewels " at the in the *Historic Royal Palaces: Tower of London* website. Accessed online at: http://www.hrp.org.uk/TowerOfLondon/stories/crownjewels

Palace, the Banqueting House, Kensington Palace and Kew Palace. Historic Royal Palaces became an Executive Agency of the Government under the Secretary of State for Culture, Media & Sport in 1989. In 1998, Historic Royal Palaces became a charitable body, although the Tower itself is owned by the Royal Armouries, an independent National Museum under the Crown. Appointed by the Crown, the Royal Constable of the Tower - a position that has existed since the earliest days of the Tower – sits on the Boards of both Historic Royal Palaces and Royal Armouries. The organization is, in essence, an autonomous extension of the Government; four of the seats are directly appointed by the Crown[83] and the other seven by the Secretary of State. [84]

As the Tower has grown in stature as a historic site, its recognition as such has also increased. In 1988, shortly before administration was taken over by Historic Royal Palaces, it was recognized by the United Nations Educational, Scientific and Cultural Organization (UNESCO) as part of its list of World Heritage Sites, a collection of humanity's finest structures[85]. It is also a "Listed" historic structure, giving it Britain's highest level of legal protection. Today it receives around 2.4 million visitors a year, with people coming from across the world to soak up almost 1,000 years of history and ambiance, brutality and beauty, fear and triumph.[86] Certainly, there are few places in the globe that have been so heavily trodden by history and those who made it, including every English king and queen since 1066, writers like Thomas Mallory, Geoffrey Chaucer and Thomas Moore, rebels like Guy Fawkes and Oliver Cromwell, foreign enemies like King John the Good and the Nazi Rudolf Hess, and countless everyday people, soldiers, servants, prisoners and tourists alike.

Buckingham Palace

Mulberry Garden and Arlington House

Ironically, Buckingham Palace's original site rails against the idea of formality. England's most well-known palace is located on a piece of land known colloquially as the Mulberry Garden, located in one of the most fashionable resorts in London and named for the trees that had been planted there by King James I. The king hoped England could use the trees to feed silk worms that could in turn make the nation less dependent on Chinese imports.

---

83 They are the Director of the Royal Collection, the Keeper of the Privy Purse, the Lord Chamberlain and the Constable of the Tower.
84 "History" at the *Historic Royal Palaces* website. Accessed online at:
    http://www.hrp.org.uk/aboutus/whoweare/history
85 "Tower of London" at the homepage of the *UNESCO World Heritage Site List*. Accessed online at:
    http://whc.unesco.org/en/list/488
86 "Historic Royal Palaces Annual Review 2010/11" accessed online at:
    http://www.hrp.org.uk/Resources/AR_WEB_2011_2.pdf

King James I of England

Ultimately, the plan proved to be a failure because the cold, wet English climate was inhospitable to silkworms, so the king graciously turned the Garden over to his people to use as a public park. However, unrest would come to England about a generation later, and on May 10, 1654, diarist John Evelyn hinted at it when he complained, "My Lady Gerrard treated us at Mulberry Gardens, now the only place of refreshment about the Town for persons of the best quality to be exceedingly cheated at: Cromwell and his partisans having shut up and closed Spring Gardens which until now had been the usual rendezvous for the Ladies and Gallants of this season." One of Evelyn's contemporaries, Samuel Pepys, called it "a silly place, with a wilderness somewhat pretty," and Clement Walker, author of *Anarchia Anglicana* (1649), suggested it was a seedy place while writing about "new-erected sodoms and spintries at the Mulberry Garden at S. James's…"

Pepys

With these and other similar complaints in mind, King Charles II decided to close the park and give the land instead to the Earl of Arlington, Henry Bennet. Historian Thomas Babington Macaulay observed that Bennet "had some talent for conversation and some for transacting ordinary business of office. He had learned during a life passed in travel and negotiating, the art of accommodating his language and deportment to the society in which he found himself. His vivacity in the closet amused the King; his gravity in debates and conferences imposed on the public, and he had succeeded in attaching to himself, partly by services, partly by hopes a considerable number of personal retainers." Likewise, the Comte de Gramont claimed that the Earl of Arlington had mastered "the gravity and solemn mien of the Spaniards, a scar across the bridge of his nose, which he covered with a little lozenge shaped plaster, gave a secretive and mysterious air to his visage [with] an overwhelming anxiety to thrust himself forward which passed for industry … and an impenetrable stupidity which passed for the power to keep a secret."

Charles II

Bennet

In his "Art of Cookery," Dr. William King observed in 1708,

> "The fate of things lies always in the dark:
> What cavalier would know St. James's Park?
> For 'Locket's' stands where gardens once did spring,
> And wild ducks quack where grasshoppers did sing:
> A princely palace on that space does rise,
> Where Sedley's noble muse found mulberries."

Arlington House seemed destined for fame from the beginning; in fact, it was here that the first cup of English tea was served. However, the house had only a short life, and in short order the house was torn down and the land on which it sat was sold to John Sheffield, the Duke of Buckingham, who built his home out more durable red brick. According to Macauley, the Duke had tried his hand at a seafaring career and like, "any lad of noble birth, any dissolute courtier, for whom one of the king's mistresses would speak a word, might hope [for] a ship of the line … If in the interval of feasting, drinking and gambling, he succeeded in learning the names of the points of the compass, he was thought fully qualified to take charge of a three decker…In 1666, John Sheffield, Earl of Mulgrave, at seventeen years of age, volunteered to serve at sea against the Dutch. He passed six weeks on board, diverting himself [with] young libertines of rank and then returned home to take command of a troop of horse. After this he was never on the water till the year 1672 when he was appointed Captain of a ship of 84 guns, reputed the finest in the navy. He was then 23 years old ... As soon as he came back from sea, he was made Colonel of a regiment of foot."

The Duke of Buckingham

Buckingham House

According to *New View of London*, (1708), Buckingham House was "a graceful palace, very commodiously situated at the westerly end of St. James's Park, having at one view a prospect of the Mall and other walks, and of the delightful and spacious canal; a seat not to be condemned by the greatest monarch...It consists of the mansion house, and at some distance from each end of that, conjoined by two arching galleries, are the lodging-rooms for servants on the south side of the court; and opposite, on the north side, are the kitchen and laundry, the fronts of which are elevated on pillars of the Tuscan, Doric, and Ionic orders, thereby constituting piazzas...The walls are brick; those of the mansion very fine rubbed and gagged, adorned with two ranges of pilasters of the Corinthian and Tuscan orders. On the latter (which are uppermost) is an acrogeria of figures, standing erect and fronting the court; they appear as big as life and look noble…The hall, partly paved with marble, is adorned with pilasters, the intercolumns are noble painture in great variety, and on a pedestal near the foot of the great staircase (whose steps are entire slabs) are the marble figures of Cain killing his brother Abel. In short, the whole structure is spacious, commodious, rich, and beautiful, but especially in the finishing and furniture. This house is now in the occupation of his Grace the Duke of Buckingham. It has a spacious court on its easterly side, fenced with a handsome wall, iron-work, and a beautiful iron gate, where the duke's coronet, arms, garter, and George are exquisitely represented in iron."

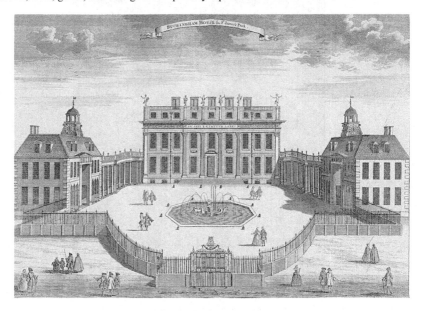

Buckingham House circa 1710

Writing toward the end of his life, the Duke himself described his residence: "I rise now in summer, about seven o'clock in a very large bedchamber (entirely quiet, high and free from the early sun) to walk in the garden or, if raining in a Salon filled with pictures, some good, but none disagreeable; There also, in a row above them, I have so many portraits of famous persons … as are enough to excite ambition in any man less lazy, or less at ease, than myself." He called his garden "the noblest that can be, presenting at once to view a vast Town, a Palace & a magnificent Cathedral…I confess myself so changed … as to my former enchanting delights, that the company I commonly find at home is agreeable enough to make me conclude the evening on a delightful Terrace. …though of more satisfaction to me than all the rest … and 'tis the little closet of books at the end of that green house which joins the best apartment, which besides their being so very near, are ranked in such a method, that by its mark a very Irish footman may fetch any book I want."

Unfortunately for Buckingham, his only legitimate son died unmarried without producing an heir, so the family lost its title in 1735. However, Buckingham's widow, Catherine Darnley, insisted on keeping the house. She was the illegitimate daughter of King James II, and historian J. H. Jesse noted one of her customs at the residence: "Here, on each successive anniversary of the execution of her grandfather, Charles I, she was accustomed to receive her company in the grand drawing-room, herself seated in a chair of state, clad in the deepest mourning, and surrounded by her women, all as black and as dismal looking as herself. Here, too, that eccentric lady breathed her last." In one of his famous letters, contemporary Horace Walpole wrote humorously, "Princess Buckingham, is either dead or dying. She sent for Mr. Anstes, and settled the ceremonial of her burial. On Saturday she was so ill that she feared dying before the pomp was come home. She said, 'Why don't they send the canopy for me to see? Let them send it, even though all the tassels are not finished.' But yesterday was the greatest stroke of all. She made her ladies vow to her that, if she should lie senseless, they would not sit down in the room before she was dead."

Fortunately, the old duke had another son, and though Charles Herbert Sheffield was born on the wrong side of the blanket, he nonetheless inherited the house after Darnley's death. He was more interested in money than his home, and in 1754 he tried to sell Buckingham House as a home for the newly established British Museum. He wrote to a trustee, "In pursuance to your commands I have considered what value to put upon my House, Gardens and Fields for which I hope if it should suit SR Hans Sloane's Trustees they won't think Thirty Thousand Pounds too much; it having cost the old Duke twice that Sum but Fifty years ago and Mr. Timbill, the Builder who was always reckoned an Honest able Man in his Profession valued it at more than [I ask] four years ago, since when I have layd out several Hundred Pounds in Repairing and Adorning it…"

Ultimately, they turned him down, so instead, Charles Herbert Sheffield sold it in 1761 to King George III for £21,000. That year, the Duke of Buckinghamshire wrote a letter to the Duke of Shrewsbury in which he described in detail the way that the exterior of Buckingham Palace looked at that time: "The avenues of this house, are along St. James's Park, through rows of good elms on one hand, and gay flourishing limes on the other; that for coaches, this for walking, with the Mall lying betwixt them. This reaches to an iron palisade that encompasses a square court, which has in the midst a great basin, with statues and water works, and from its entrance rises all the way imperceptibly, till we mount to a terrace in the front of a large ball, paved with square white stones, mixed with a dark colored marble…."

King George III

The duke also described the interior, writing that "on the right hand, we go into a parlour thirty-three feet by thirty-nine, with a niche fifteen feet broad for a beaufet, paved with white marble, and placed within an arch, with pilasters of divers colors, the upper part of which, as high as the ceiling, is painted by Ricci. From hence we pass through a suite of large rooms into a bedchamber of thirty-four feet by twenty-seven; within it a large closet that opens into a green-house…On the left hand of the hall are three stone arches, supported by three Corinthian pillars, under one of which we go up forty-eight steps, ten feet broad, each step of one entire Portland stone. These stairs, by the help of two resting places, are so very easy there is no need of leaning on the iron baluster…. the largeness of the whole had admitted of a sure remedy against any decay of the colors from saltpeter in the wall, by making another of oak laths four inches within it, and so primed over like a picture."

According to Buckinghamshire, the stairs ended on the second floor just outside double doors that opened into a large salon. There were a number of other rooms upstairs, several reached by what he called "great doors."

Fortunately for both the royal and common members of the household, the house was not designed simply to be beautiful but also to be functional. For one thing, the passages from the kitchen and to the cellars were covered so that the servants could carry out their work even in inclement weather. There were also two back staircases that allowed the servants to come and go upstairs without disturbing their masters, and without having to deal with running into them. The kitchen was also well designed for use and comfort, with 30 feet high ceilings and a cupola on top that dissipated the heat and odors that otherwise might have accumulated there. The larder and laundry were located near the kitchen.

On top of the palace roof was a lead cistern. A large pump kept this full of water from the Thames River, and according to Buckinghamshire, it held up to 12,500 gallons of water that was used for everything except drinking. Instead, the royals and their servants drank the beer brewed in the palace brew house, which was also located near the kitchen.

Once he purchased the property, the king naturally furnished it with the best items money could buy. To that end, he commissioned Vile & Cobb, master furniture makers. According to biographer J. T. Smith, Mr. Cobb was "a singularly haughty man, the upholsterer. One of the proudest men in England, he always appeared in full dress of the most superb and costly kind, whether strutting magnificently through his workshops, giving orders to his men, or on some errand at the 'Queen's House', where the King who smiled at his pomposity frequently employed him for cabinet work of an elaborate and expensive sort…His Majesty's library at the Queen's House when giving orders to a workman whose ladder chanced to stand before a book required by the King, His Majesty desired Cobb to hand him the work. Instead of obeying, Cobb called to his man, 'fellow, give me that book!' The King with his usual condescension rose and asked Cobb for his man's name. 'Jenkins, your Majesty,' answered the astonished upholsterer. 'Then,' observed the King, 'Jenkins. You shall hand me that book.'"

King George III also enjoyed purchasing fine furniture previously owned by others, as another writer reported: "On Monday his Majesty passed by West Thorpe House near Marlow, the seat of the late Governor Winch. He sent one of his Equerries to enquire whose goods were selling by auction; when Mr. Christie requested his most dutiful respects might be presented to his Majesty for he wished to show him some very curious ivory chairs and a couch that were to be disposed of." Could this be Mr. Christie of the soon to be famous auction house? The author continued, "His Majesty turned back, they were shown him on the lawn opposite the house and he liked them so well that he ordered them to be purchased for the Queen … the chairs cost 14½ guineas each, the couch 48 guineas and two small cabinets 45 guineas."

On March 23, 1767, Mrs. Philip Lybbe Powys described her visit to Buckingham: "The hall and staircase are particularly pleasing. The whole of the ground floor is for the King, whose apartments are fitted up rather neatly elegant than profusely ornamental. The library consists of three rooms, two oblong and one octagonal. The books are said to be the best collection anywhere to be met with…The Queen's apartments are ornamented as one expects a Queen's should be, with curiosities from every nation that can deserve her notice. The most capital pictures, the finest Dresden & other china, cabinets of more minute curiosities. Among the pictures let us note the famed cartoons from Hampton Court & a number of small & beautiful pictures; one room panelled with the finest Japan. The floors are all inlaid in the most expensive manner, and tho' but in March, every room was full of Roses, carnations, hyacinths etc, dispersed in the prettiest manner imaginable in jars & different flowerpots on stands. On her toilet, besides the gilt plate, innumerable knick-knacks…Round the dressing room, let into the crimson damask hangings in a manner uncommonly elegant, are frames of fine impressions, miniatures etc. It being at that time the coldest weather possible we were amazed to find so large a house so warm but fires, it seems, are kept the whole day, even in the closets, and to prevent accidents to furniture so costly from the neglect of the attendance, there is in every chimney a lacquered wire fire board, the cleverest contrivance that can be imagin'd as even the smallest spark cannot fly through them, while you have the heat & they are really ornamental."

In the years that followed, Buckingham House, as it was still known, was the site of more births than deaths. "Mad King George" and his wife had more than a dozen children, and as time passed, they became so enamored of the house that they decided to make it their permanent home, leaving St. James Palace to be used only for formal occasions of state. In 1775, Parliament formerly ceded Buckingham, not to George III, as might be assumed, but to his devoted wife, Queen Charlotte, in exchange for her giving up her home at Somerset House. Therefore, Buckingham House soon came to be known as the "Queen's House."

Queen Charlotte

Around the same time, in 1773, one Englishman described the house in less than glowing terms, writing, "In the front it is enclosed with a semi-circular sweep of iron rails, which are altered very unhappily from the rails which enclosed it before it became a royal residence. Formerly an elegant pair of gates opened in the middle; but now, though a foot-opening leads up to where an opening naturally is expected in front, all entrance is forbidden, by the rails being oddly continued across without affording an avenue through. Whoever seeks to enter must walk round either to the right or left, and in the corners perhaps he may gain admittance…The edifice is a mixture of brick and stone, with a broad flight of steps leading up to the door, which is between four tall Corinthian pilasters, which are fluted and reach up to the top of the second storey. ... Behind the house is a garden and terrace, from which there is a fine prospect of the adjacent country."

About 25 years later, another author was more charitable, noting that Buckingham Palace "contains within apartments as spacious and commodious as any palace in Europe for state parade." Also, when the Prince of Wales, the future King George IV, married, "a suite of the principal rooms was fitted up in the most splendid manner; the walls of two of the levee rooms being hung with beautiful tapestry, then recently discovered with its colors unfaded in an old chest at St. James's...In the grand levee room, is a bed of crimson velvet, manufactured in Spitalfields. The canopy of the throne likewise is of crimson velvet, trimmed with broad gold lace, and embroidered with crowns set with fine pearls of great value. This was first used on Queen Charlotte's birthday, after the union of the kingdoms of Great Britain and Ireland, and the shamrock, the badge of the Irish nation, is interwoven with the other decorations of the crown with peculiar taste and propriety."

George IV

There was an unusual, octagonal apartment located in the southeast corner of the palace. Housed there was one of the premier collections of cartoons drawn by the famed Renaissance artist Raphael. There was also a throne room where Queen Charlotte received her most important visitors. However, for the most part, the future palace remained, as architect William Henry Leeds observed in 1838, "dull, dowdy, and decent; nothing more than a large, substantial, and respectable-looking red brick house; quite unsophisticated in its appearance, with the exception that it was garnished in the center with four Corinthian stone pilasters in a taste partaking more of the Dutch than the classical style…never the less such intermixture of brick and stone has been regarded rather as a beauty than otherwise by one critic, M. Quatremere de Roissy, who gives it as his opinion that red brick serving as a ground to columns and entablatures, sets them off to greater advantage. Most certainly such contrast of color and material does render the stone dressings more conspicuous, and where it is in unison with the style employed, such intermixture of material may be resorted to with advantage: but wherever orders — either Greek or Italian are employed, the effect is apt to be harsh and crude, as well as to partake of meanness."

No matter how the palace looked architecturally, it was still the home of the sovereigns, which ensured that it continued to attract the most prominent Englishmen, including those who enjoyed creating things of beauty. For instance, one artist wrote to a friend in 1770, "Last Monday, Mr. Wedgwood and I had a long audience of their Majesties, at the Queen's palace, to present some bas-reliefs which the Queen had ordered, and to show some new improvements, with which they were well pleased. They expressed in the most obliging and condescending manner their attention to our manufacture, and entered very freely into conversation on the further improvements of it, and on many other subjects." Of course, this was Wedgwood of china fame.

In 1779, a serious storm blew through London and seriously damaged Buckingham House. Mrs. Papendiek, whose father was a page at court, later recalled, "It took off the upper corner of the Queen's House. This was the room next to the one in which the Princes Ernest, Augustus & Adolphus slept, which was over the bedroom of their majesties. The King was up, and with his children in a moment. The ceiling was falling fast & had already already broken the bedstead of the elder Prince … but no harm happened to them." This incident forced the already busy king to pay more attention to his home, a problem he did not need in the middle of the American Revolution.

In addition to the trouble across the Atlantic, the late 18th century was a turbulent time in Europe, especially in England, where King George III was trying to fight wars on multiple fronts. In 1780, when riots broke out in London, George was forced to use Buckingham House as a fortress, clearly something it was never intended to be. He established the Queen's Riding House as a sort of command center, and one contemporary reported, "Between three and four thousand troops were in the Queen's Gardens, and surrounded Buckingham House. During the first night the alarm was so sudden, that no straw could be got for the troops to rest themselves on; which being told his Majesty, he, accompanied with one or two officers, went throughout the ranks..." According to the writer, the king said, "My lads, my crown cannot purchase you straw to-night; but depend on it, I have given orders that a sufficiency shall be here to-morrow forenoon; as a substitute for the straw, my servants will instantly serve you with a good allowance of wine and spirits, to make your situation as comfortable as possible; and I shall keep you company myself till morning." The report went on to say, "The King did so, walking mostly in the garden, sometimes visiting the Queen and the children in the palace, and receiving all messages in the Riding House, it being in a manner head-quarters. When he was told that part of the mob was attempting to get into St. James's Palace, he forbade the soldiers to fire, but ordered them to keep off the rioters with their bayonets."

Such actions made King George III popular with the common people, and his parties made him popular with his courtiers. In 1786, Sophie von la Roche recounted her visit to Buckingham House: "The noble simplicity of the furnishings, the order and neatness, were marks of the character of the owner – marks of the wise humility upon the throne. The library occupies the largest apartment and embraces the entire treasure-house of human knowledge. Three rooms are given up to it…Fine pictures by Van Dyck, a large number by Claude Lorrain, Guido Reni, Del Sarto, masterpieces by Angelica [Kauffmann] and some excellent miniatures render these simple damask hangings very valuable. In a small cabinet off the bedroom are the portraits of the fourteen royal children – thus the first waking moments are dedicated to this sight and the emotions of true motherhood…The concert hall contains a large organ…because the royal family holds private prayers to an organ accompaniment; for it has always been mainly associated with church music. The audience chamber is devoid of all splendour: one cabinet, however, is enhanced by the queen's tapestry-work. In a side room looking on to the garden an artist was at work; and there, too, we found two lovely portraits of the youngest princesses…There is a colonnade in the vestibule worthy of the dignity of this small palace's mistress…since the stairs are also decorated with frescoes … The choice of site for this palace is perfect, as it takes in the gradual incline, from which the royal park of St James's and Green Park can be completely overlooked, and at the back of it a pleasant garden has been laid out in which to take a solitary stroll."

She concluded by quoting Mr. Vulliamy, who said, "The eye of the queen spreads this elegance in Buckingham's house, just as her heart allows the king to savour the sweet happiness of purest love."

The 19th Century

Unfortunately, the entertainments held there were often far more elegant than their surroundings, for in the early years of the 19th century, as King George III began his descent into madness, Buckingham House once again fell into disrepair. In 1802, a reporter from the *Gentleman's Magazine* observed that the floors were "cold and hardrubbed…without a carpet, a luxury of which his majesty denies himself in almost every room." Attempting to improve her surroundings, one of the many princesses living in the household had painted (or perhaps more accurately, dyed) the velvet curtains "in shades of brown and maroon." However, the furniture remained "very plain and old fashion," made of materials that were "not always so … good, seldom so beautiful as would be required in the houses of many opulent individuals. Though old, the furniture bears no stamp of venerable antiquity. The damask of the curtains and chairs is much faded: the mahogany … is not beautiful: it is even so dull that it much resembles walnut; and the latter are made with curving legs, and clump or rather knob feet, not well carved."

In 1811, a Scottish artist, Charles Kirkpatrick Sharpe, complained to Lady Charlotte Campbell, "I was one of the happy few at H 's ball given in B--m House — a house I had been long anxious to see, as it is rendered classical by the pen of Pope and the pencil of Hogarth. It is in a woeful condition, and, as I hear, to be pulled down. The company was very genteel (I can't get a less vulgar word to express the sort of things) and very dull; but all the ladies were vastly refreshed with an inscription chalked upon the floor, which each applied to herself. Within a wreath of laurel, like burdock, fastened with fifty crooked true-love knots, were the mysterious words 'Pour elle.'"

Sharpe

In the 19th century, as in the 21st century, Buckingham Palace was used to impress upon visitors the importance and grandeur of the English monarchy. For instance, in 1809, when the Ambassador from Persia visited, the English were more than a little anxious to make a good impression, being still unfamiliar with the ways of the Far East. Thus, according to the records, when he arrived, "the great iron gates fronting the park were thrown open for his entrance."

One of the most long-lasting changes brought to English society began with Queen Charlotte, who wanted her children to enjoy the types of Christmas decorations she had had in her youth in Germany. Among these was a Christmas tree, an innovation among the British, who had never before had such an item. One courtier remembered, "It was hung with presents for the children, who were invited to see it; and I well remember the pleasure that it was to hunt for one's own name, which was sure to be attached to one or more of the pretty gifts."

By this time, much about the palace had changed, and the fourth volume of "The Ladies Cabinet of Fashion, Music and Nature" noted the changes made since Buckinghamshire's time: "The 'goodly elms and gay flourishing limes' went to decay. The 'iron palisade' assumed a more modern form; and of the 'great basin with statues and waterworks' no traces were left. Many of these statues were deposited in the famous lead statue yard, in Piccadilly; but that also in its turn ceased to exist; what became of the images we have not learnt. The terrace mentioned by the Duke was entirely done away, and the entrance came to be those small steps into the hall...The 'covered passage from the kitchen' was built up; the 'corridors supported on Ionic pillars' were filled in with brick work. and more modern door-ways, windows with compartments over them, inserted therein, with strings. plinth, &c., constituting concealed passages from the wings to the house. The Duke's 'kitchen, with an open cupola at top,' was at length nowhere to be found. The renovated plan, as seen externally, continued to be nearly the same, with the exception of the palisade, great basin, covered passages, the building up of the corridors, terrace, or flight of steps, and an additional door-way to the left wing...Festoons of flowers and fruit, which were under the windows of the principal floor, were cut out, and in their place the side balustrades remained in continuation. Sills of three mouldings only remained under the windows of the principal floor; a continued string occupied their place to the hall story; to the attic floor, architraves to the four sides of the windows of the wings common cills were given, &c. &c."

George III died in 1820 and was succeeded by his son, George IV. A few years into his reign, the new king, who loved to live lavishly, set about expanding the palace and making major renovations to both the interior and exterior of the building. The king chose John Nash, then the Official Architect to the Office of Woods and Forests, to head the work. Nash later wrote, "His late Majesty's intentions and commands were to convert Buckingham House into a private residence for himself. A plan was made upon a small scale, merely adding a few rooms to the old house. Whilst this plan was forming, and on my observing that the plan was being enlarged, I continually urged his Majesty to build in some other situation, and made several plans for that purpose, using all the arguments in my power to dissuade his Majesty from adding to the old Palace, but without any effect; for the late King constantly persisted that he would not build a new Palace, but would add to the present house."

Undeterred, he continued, "I then urged his Majesty to pull down the house, and rebuild it higher up in the garden in a line with Pall Mall. To induce his Majesty's acquiescence, I stated the lowness of the present site and the northern aspect, and recommended that the house should be placed on a level with Hyde Park Corner, and in a line with Pall Mall, a road or prolongation of which should cross the Green Park as an approach. This proposition I thought had some weight, and for a time I had hopes my recommendation would be adopted...."

He soon learned that the king would not be so easily swayed, especially when the sovereign said to another high ranking official in his presence, "Long, now remember I tell Nash before you at his peril, ever to advise me to build a palace. I am too old to build a palace, I have no objection to build one, but I must have a pied à terre. I do not like Carlton House standing in a street; and, moreover, I tell him I will have it at Buckingham House; and if he pulls it down he shall rebuild it in the same place; there are early associations which endear me to the spot."

Nash finally acquiesced. According to the Royal Trust, which today supervises the maintenance of Buckingham Palace, "During the last five years of George IV's life, Nash enlarged Buckingham House into the imposing U-shaped building which was to become Buckingham Palace. ... He extended the central block of the building westwards and to the north and south, and the two wings to the east were entirely rebuilt. The wings enclosed a grand forecourt which transformed the aspect of the Palace from St James's Park...Nash also created a triumphal arch in the center of the forecourt. The arch formed part of a ceremonial processional approach to the Palace and celebrated Britain's recent naval and military victories."

Nash

During this period, a popular ditty rose up concerning the newly improved palace. It went, in part:

> This is the Entrance, the Triumphal Arch,
>
> Which, 'tis said, will be probably finish'd in March,
>
> (And, compared with the elegant gates of Hyde Park,
>
> May justly be term'd tasteless, gloomy, and dark,)
>
> Which leads to the large Pond of Water, or Basin,
>
> Where the Royal Narcissus may see his dear face in,

Ere he rove 'mong the Pyramids, Temples, and Ditches,

Where Naiads and Cupids are seen without breeches,

(For such things in the West are allow'd, and thought pretty.

Though Venus and Cupids daren't go in the City,)

Who preside o'er the Fountains, the Promenades, and Rides,

(And 'twould puzzle old Harry to tell what besides,)

Which lead from the Hill, the magnificent Mound,

Thrown up in the Garden, full half a mile round.

To protect from the breeze and to hide from the people

Thickly planted with trees, and as high as a steeple,

These much-talk'd-of wings which by estimate round

Are said to have cost forty-two thousand pound.

And which not quite according with Royalty's taste.

Are doom'd to come down and be laid into waste;

(So to make up the loss of such changing and chopping,

The pay of poor clerks they're eternally docking,)

But they touch not the beautiful Ball in the Cup,

Which the tasteful Committee in wisdom set up

On the top of the Palace that N--H built.

The people's complaints were understandable, as the Royal Trust explained: "The Buckingham Palace created by Nash was widely regarded as a masterpiece. It came, however, at a considerable cost. By 1828 Nash had spent £496,169 on the changes to the building. Soon after the death of George IV two years later, the Prime Minister...dismissed Nash from his post for over-spending. Lord Duncannon, First Commissioner of Works, took over the task of overseeing the completion of the Palace. Duncannon appointed a new architect in Edward Blore, who extended the east façade at both ends and created a new entrance (the Ambassadors' Entrance) on the southern side. ...the State Rooms were completed between 1833 and 1834."

An engraving depicting Buckingham Palace in the 1830s

As it turned out, King William IV, who succeeded his brother as king in 1830, had no desire to live in the palace and instead remained where he was in Clarence House. In fact, when fire severely damaged the Houses of Parliament in 1834, he offered Buckingham Palace as a replacement, assuring Parliament that he had no need for it. Parliament's leaders decided against taking over the former home of royalty and instead authorized sufficient funding to have the building properly completed for a royal home. This move proved very providential, because the string of old kings was about to give way to a young queen who would make her home there for much of the 19th Century.

King William IV

It is unlikely that anybody ever moved into Buckingham Palace with as much enthusiasm and joy as did the young Queen Victoria in 1837. She had grown up in Kensington Palace, which was by no means dreary, but her life there was, as she lived under the constant scrutiny of her mother and her mother's unscrupulous advisor, John Conroy. Victoria later recalled, "My earliest recollections are connected with Kensington Palace, where I can remember crawling on a yellow carpet spread out for that purpose -- and being told that if I cried and was naughty my 'Uncle Sussex' would hear me and punish me, for which reason I always screamed when I saw him! ... I used to ride a donkey given me by my Uncle, the Duke of York, who was very kind to me. ... To Tunbridge Wells we also went, living at a house called Mt. Pleasant, now an Hotel. Many pleasant days were spent here, and the return to Kensington in October or November was generally a day of tears."

Victoria as a teen

Victoria's mother, the Duchess of Kent

Biographer Kate Williams described these early years: "The duchess and Conroy attempted to bend Victoria to their will with a plan known as the 'Kensington system'. According to Victoria's half brother, Prince Charles of Leiningen, 'the basis of all actions, of the whole system followed at Kensington' was to ensure that the duchess had such influence over her daughter that 'the nation should have to assign her the regency', and the people would always associate her with Victoria. The aim was to make certain that 'nothing and no one should be able to tear the daughter away from her' … The Kensington system involved constant surveillance of the little girl 'down to the smallest and most insignificant detail'. Every cough, every piece of bread and butter consumed, every stamp of the tiny foot was reported to Conroy. The princess was forbidden the company of other children, and was never left alone. Although there were plenty of rooms, she slept in her mother's chamber and her governess sat with her until the duchess came to bed." In 1843, when she had been married for a few years to her beloved Albert and was herself a mother, Victoria admitted "that certainly my Kensington life for the last six or seven years had been one of great misery and oppression…"

Prince Albert

For the still young Victoria, Buckingham Palace symbolized freedom and a new life for herself, and what a life it was during those first carefree years of her reign, as she threw herself into enjoying all the pleasures that had been denied her as a girl. She had very little interest in the palace itself, other than as a backdrop for entertaining, and it was only later, after she married Prince Albert in 1840, that any real efforts were made to further improve the palace.

For all their great love for each other, Albert and Victoria were in many ways opposites. That extended to interior decorating; while she paid no attention to their home whatsoever, he was obsessed with every small detail of how the house operated. Accustomed as he was to German efficiency, he was appalled at the way the maintenance of his new home was handled. Under the supervision of Victoria's former governess, Baroness Louise Lehzen, the house was always dusty, and servants were allowed to do their jobs in a lax manner. In one of the most famous legends of the palace at that time, Albert asked his young wife why the windows were always dirty, and she replied airily that one team washed the insides while another washed the outsides and that they were never in sync.

Lehzen

Then there was the matter of security. In March 1841, a young man known as "the boy Jones" managed to break into the palace and roam the halls for some time before being caught. To make matters worse, this happened on more than one occasion. Writing in the *Journal*, a Mr. Raikes noted, "A little scamp of an apothecary's errand-boy, named Jones, has the unaccountable mania of sneaking privately into Buckingham Palace, where he is found secreted at night under a sofa, or some other hiding-place close to the Queen's bed-chamber. No one can divine his object, but twice he has been detected and conveyed to the police-office, and put into confinement for a time. The other day he was detected in a third attempt, with apparently as little object. Lady Sandwich wittily wrote that he must undoubtedly be a descendant of In-I-Go Jones, the architect."

In spite of these and other problems, Victoria's early years at Buckingham Palace were happy ones, and they set the tone for the future. Indeed, the elegant home became the backdrop for multiple births and marriages. In 1840, Victoria provided the country with an heir who bore her own name, and the following year, the infant Princess Victoria was supplanted in more ways than one by her brother, Bertie, who would become the future King Edward VII. To date, King Edward VII is the only monarch to both be born and die in Buckingham Palace, although it is possible in the future that he could be joined by his great-great-grandson, the current Prince Charles, who was also born there.

King Edward VII

In 1843, Victoria's cousin, Princess Augusta of Cambridge, married Frederick William, Grand Duke of Mecklenburg-Strelitz. Always anxious that her beloved husband should receive the respect he was due, and then some, she nearly made a scene at the wedding. Again, Raikes reported the story, told to him by the Duke of Wellington: "When we proceeded to the signatures of the bride and bridegroom, the King of Hanover was very anxious to sign before Prince Albert, and when the Queen approached the table, he placed himself by her side, watching his opportunity. She knew very well what he was about, and just as the Archbishop was giving her the pen, she suddenly dodged round the table, placed herself next to the Prince, then quickly took the pen from the Archbishop, signed, and gave it to Prince Albert, who also signed next, before it could be prevented."

The wedding may have been held in the new private chapel, completed that same year. The pious monarchs ordered it built in a comfortable space formerly occupied by a conservatory.

This was the first of a number of building projects commissioned in the years that followed, and by the time they were done, Victoria and her husband spent more than £150,000 renovating the east side of the building. The work took place under the watchful eye of architect Edward Blore, and so much was done that by 1851, Nash himself might not have recognized his own work. Most significantly, Blore moved Nash's famous Marble Arch from the palace's main entrance to the northeast corner of Hyde Park. While it had once displayed a banner indicating that the sovereign was in residence, that role was passed on to a flagpole sitting atop the palace itself.

Blore

In 1883, Noel Ruthven noted, "The new east front of the palace is the same length as the garden front; the height to top of the balustrade is nearly eighty feet, and it has a central and two arched side entrances, leading direct into the quadrangle. The wings are surmounted by statues representing 'Morning,' 'Noon,' and 'Night;' the 'Hours and the Seasons;' and upon turrets, flanking the central shield (bearing 'V. R. 1847'), are colossal figures of 'Britannia' and 'St. George;' besides groups of trophies, festoons of flowers, &c. Around the entire building is a scroll frieze of the rose, shamrock, and thistle."

Furthermore, he complained, "It has been asserted that the mismanagement on the part of the

Government nearly ruined the artist of the magnificent gates of the arch. Their cost was 3,000 guineas, and they are the largest and most superb in Europe, not excepting the stupendous gates of the Ducal Palace at Venice, and those made by order of Buonaparte for the Louvre at Paris. Yet the Government agents are reported to have conveyed these costly gates from the manufacturer's in a 'common stage wagon,' when the semi-circular head, the most beautiful portion of the design, was irretrievably mutilated; and, consequently, it has not been fixed in the archway to the present day."

At the same time, he wrote about some of the palace's more prominent features: "The most important portions of the palace are the Marble Hall and Sculpture Gallery, the Library, the Grand Staircase, the Vestibule, the state apartments, consisting of the New Drawing-room, and the Throne-room, the Picture Gallery (where her present Majesty has placed a valuable collection of paintings), the Grand Saloon, and the State Ballroom."

Members of the Royal Family with President Richard Nixon in the Marble Hall

Queen Elizabeth II with the First Couple in one of the private apartments in the north wing of the palace

The Queen's Gallery

According to Ruthven, the Entrance-hall was surrounded by double columns, each with gilded bases and capitals and all standing one base. He observed that each column consisted of one piece of Carrara marble and that the Grand Staircase, carved of white marble, was elaborately decorated. It, and much of the State Ballroom, was decorated by L. Gruner at a cost of around £300,000. Here, Victoria ordered hung the state portraits made of her and Albert by Winterhalter. They appeared during her reign alongside those of the doomed Charles I and his wife, Henrietta Maria.

The Library, which also served as a waiting-room for deputations, was "decorated in a manner combining comfort with elegance" and opened onto the terrace. From its windows one could see the chapel at one end and the conservatory at the other. But of course, the real beauty lay in its view of the gardens. Once those granted an audience with Her Majesty left this room, they passed through the Sculpture Gallery, where busts of important statesmen were housed, as well as those of members of the Royal Family, and into the Hall. Next, they proceeded up the Grand Staircase through another ante-room and into the Green Drawing Room, their last stop before the Throne Room itself. The Green Drawing Room opened onto the upper floor of the porch running along the old part of the building. It was, apparently, "a long and lofty apartment." Those not visiting the palace for an audience passed through the Green Drawing-room to the Picture Gallery or the Grand Saloon. Not surprisingly, the former housed some of the very finest pieces of art from the day and earlier, including works by Dutch and Flemish artists, as well as those of the Italian and English schools. The Picture Gallery itself was nearly 150 feet long and 150 feet wide and lighted by skylights which, while providing the area with excellent light, wreaked havoc on the paintings themselves.

The Throne Room, of course, was the most dreamed of destination, and it ran along the eastern side of the building for more than sixty feet. During Victoria's time, the walls were hung with crimson red satin and velvet, and the ceiling was richly carved and gilded. However, in Ruthven's mind, of all the more than 700 rooms in the palace, the Yellow Drawing Room was thought to be the most magnificent, for it featured elaborately carved furniture, much of which was overlaid with burnished gold and upholstered with broad-striped yellow satin. Located just outside the Queen's private apartments, its ceiling was supported by several polished marble pillars standing against the four walls, each of which featured a full-length portrait of a member of the Royal Family.

Near the Yellow Drawing Room lay the saloon, right at the center of the garden front. Ruthven described it as "superbly decorated," with purple scagliolan Corinthian columns carved to look like lapis lazuli. He insisted that "the entablature, cornice, and ceiling are profusely enriched; and the remaining decorations and furniture are of corresponding magnificence." Meanwhile, the South Drawing Room featured "compositions in relief," including those of Spenser,

Shakespeare, and Milton.

For the vast majority of people who will never see the inside of Buckingham Palace, the State Dining Room holds perhaps that most appeal, with its long table and rows of gilded chairs. Ruthven himself considered it "a very spacious and handsome apartment," pointing to the long row of windows that ran alongside and overlooked the garden. Between each window hung a long mirror designed to increase the light in the room. The ceiling was carved with "foliage and floral ornamentation" and portraits of deceased royals ran the length of the other side of the room.

The gardens at Buckingham Palace were never going to rival those at Kensington, but, as Horace Walpole observed, "The garden, or west front, of the palace, architecturally the principal one, has five Corinthian towers, and also a balustraded terrace, on the upper portion of which are statues, trophies, and bas-reliefs, by Flaxman and other distinguished sculptors. The pleasure grounds cover a space of about forty acres, five of which are occupied by a lake. Upon the summit of a lofty artificial mound, rising from the margin of the lake, is a picturesque pavilion, or garden-house, with a minaret roof. In the center is an octagonal room..."

On the north side of the garden lay the Royal Mews, or stables. There, each of Victoria's nine children took riding lessons, and there also were housed her more than 40 carriages, including the still famous State Coach designed by Sir William Chambers in 1762 and painted by Cipriani.

In 1851, Queen Victoria, or more precisely, her children, made history and set a new precedent when they became the first members of the Royal Family to appear on the balcony of Buckingham Palace during a public celebration. As Queen Victoria and Prince Albert left in procession to open the Great Exhibition, "a groundbreaking showcase of international manufacturing, masterminded by Prince Albert," the *London Daily News* reported, "At this moment the new front of the palace was put to a use never contemplated by those who have been so eager in their enunciation of the architect. The many windows gave to her Majesty's household the opportunity they never before enjoyed so perfectly of catalogue: seeing a state procession. The balcony over the center bronzed gateway was occupied by a most interesting party—the younger children of the royal the royal family, attended by several ladies."

The older members of the Royal Family appeared again on the balcony on March 1, 1854. The *London Express* reported, "The first battalion of the Scot Fusilier Guards paraded in front of Buckingham Palace at 7 o'clock yesterday morning, immediately after leaving the Wellington Barracks en route to Portsmouth, for embarkation on foreign service. Her Majesty, Prince Albert, the Prince of Wales, Prince Alfred, and the Princesses appeared on the balcony of the center window. The battalion, under the command of Colonel Dixon, being formed in line, presented arms, and gave three cheers, after which they marched to the Waterloo station on the South Western Railway."

The observation had been accurately made that Buckingham Palace is like a duck, sailing serenely across the water while its feet paddle frantically beneath the surface. While they are not typically frantic, those paddling beneath the surface in Victoria's day included hundreds of servants, led by the "Board of Green Cloth," a five member leadership team made up of the Lord Steward, the Treasurer, the Comptroller, the Master of the Household, and the Secretary. Together these five supervised the many separate departments of the royal household. According to Murray, writing in his *Official Handbook of Church and State*, "The Lord Steward of the Household…is the chief officer of the Queen's Household, all the officers and servants of which are under his control, except those belonging to the Chapel, the Chamber, and the Stable. His authority extends over the offices of Treasurer, Comptroller, and Master of the Household. The Lord Steward is at the head of the Court of the Queen's Household—the Board of Green Cloth. He is always sworn a member of the Privy Council. He has precedence before all peers of his own degree. He has no formal grant of his office, but receives his charge immediately from the Queen by the delivery of his white staff of office…He holds his appointment during pleasure, and his tenure depends upon the political party of which he is a member. … The Lord Steward has the selection and appointment of all the subordinate officers and servants of the Household, and also of the Queen's tradesmen, except those connected with the royal stables…The Treasurer of the Household acts for the Lord Steward in his absence. … The Comptroller is subordinate to the two preceding officers, for whom he acts in their absence. … His particular duty consists in the examination and check of the Household expenses. … The Master of the Household stands next in rank to this department. He is an officer under the Treasurer, and examines a portion of the accounts; but his duties consist more especially in superintending the selection, qualification, and conduct of the Household servants."

Modern History

Many royal households have been the sites of births and deaths, illnesses and recoveries, but only Buckingham Palace has hosted not one but two major operations performed upon a sitting monarch. The first took place on June 21, 1902, on the recently crowned Edward VII. The first word that there was trouble came that afternoon, when the palace announced simply, "King Edward is suffering from perityphlitis [appendicitis] and is undergoing a surgical operation." Then, on the 24th, the people were informed, "The operation has been successfully performed. A large abscess has been evacuated The king has borne the operation well and is in a satisfactory condition."

Encouraging bulletins continued to be posted, and the *Associated Press* eventually reported, "The King's doctors believe that his majesty would have been dead before now except for the operation. His condition became so alarming last night that at one time it was feared death might ensue before the surgeon's knife could afford him relief. Intense swelling of the-extremities, accompanied by alarming symptoms of mortification, constituted the emergency which demanded an immediate operation. To the last the king tried to avoid this, and he was willing to be carried to the abbey for the coronation ceremony, in order that it should occur as arranged…The influence of Queen Alexandra was enlisted, however, and at an early hour this morning the royal patient was prepared for the operation, which, even in the skillful hands of England's best surgeons, was fraught with grave danger. Shortly before 2 o'clock this afternoon his majesty was moved from his couch to the operating table and the anesthetic was administered. Sir Frederick Treves made the incision, near the patient's groin and carried it upwards, with an outward slant, for nearly four inches. The obstruction was removed and a tubing was placed in the affected intestine."

The second operation, performed in September 1951, was less successful, even though it occurred after medical science had advanced by nearly 50 years. King George VI was operated on in the hope that removing his lung might stop the spread of the cancer that had recently been diagnosed. The *Associated Press* reported on September 24, "The brief announcement said 'The king has had a restful night. His majesty's condition this morning continues to be as satisfactory aa can be expected.' It came after a Buckingham Palace source had reported that the king 'made it safely' through the first crucial night after his operation yesterday morning, Anxious Britons, who had prayed for the safety of their beloved monarch, got no indication of the king's exact condition in his battle the after effects of the surgery. … Handwritten with soft lead pencil the bulletin was posted on a board attached to the fence in front of Buckingham Palace."

King George VI

In sickness and in health, the peopled gathered at the palace gates. The article continued, "A tall police inspector read the bulletin aloud over the heads of the jostling throng. People then lined up and filed slowly past for a firsthand look. … Medical authorities are in general agreement that the first four or five days after the operation are the crucial period. As the sovereign fought his lonely battle for life, a little group of Britons kept a prayerful vigil outside the gates of massive Buckingham Palace…They were joined after daybreak by persons on their way to work who stopped to ask "How is he," very much like old friends asking after a neighbor. Others, set for a longer wait in hopes of new medical bulletins on the king's condition, parked their cars in the mall near the palace or sat quietly around the nearby monument to Queen Victoria."

The public would only learn the exact nature of the king's surgery after his death a few months later in February 1952.

For all the many people throughout the centuries who have admired and held the Royal Family in the highest esteem, not everyone who has gathered in front of Buckingham Palace did so to see them or wish them well. For instance, in 1914, 20,000 women marched there to demand the right to vote in local and parliamentary elections. The press was not particularly impressed, as the *Telegraph* made clear when it told readers that the incident was a "serious fracas between the wild women and the police, in which the militants delivered a brief but furious attack on the constables." The article added that Emmeline Pankhurst, the leader of the group, "was able to offer little or no resistance, but shouting out that she had got to the palace gates, she was carried bodily by a chief inspector to a private motor which the police had in waiting."

Pankhurst

The protest made news around the world, with the *Associated Press* reporting, "While leading an army of women upon Buckingham palace. Mrs. Emmeline Pankhurst, leader of the militant suffragettes, was arrested. Immediately after King George and Queen Mary arrived from

Aldershot, where they have been for five days inspecting the great military establishment, the women gathered at Whitehall and moved toward Buckingham palace. … Their majesties, however, had stolen a march upon the suffragettes, for, instead of going direct to Buckingham palace, upon their arrival they went to Marlborough house, the residence of Dowager Queen Alexandra…More than 2,000 policemen, detectives and soldiers were on duty in the streets and around the palace to prevent rioting. Home Secretary McKenna had sent word to the leaders of the women that King George would not receive them under any circumstances. but this did not deter them "If he won't see us we will see him," was the reply sent back to the home secretary. … As Mrs. Pankhurst was being taken to Holloway jail she lost all control of herself. With blazing eyes she struggled in the grasp of the police men. meanwhile shrieking, "That's right; arrest me at the gates of the king. Go tell the king you have arrested me."

The women's demands were largely overshadowed by the economic condition in England, a situation that continued to be a problem in the early days of World War I. In September 1914, *The Times* reported that "the beginning of extensive interior decoration work at the palace has been hastened by the Queen's desire … to give employment to a class of workmen who will be the first to feel the pinch of retrenchment owing to the war. Alterations include a large quantity of parquet flooring specially made by Messrs. Howard of Berners St., a class of work hitherto much in the hands of German makers."

Much of the work done at this time was on the queen's private apartments and Charles Allom, director of White Allom, praised her taste, especially the way in which she designed her bedroom. In *Decorative artists to the King and Queen*, he wrote, "The room has been structurally altered by throwing the private service corridor into it, and this has led to the occurrence of an unusual feature. The fireplace is left in the centre of the wall, (the openings in which are supported by columns) which was pierced to open up the corridor now utilized for a long range of wardrobes." He further praised the "soft color that enables it to blend charmingly with the furniture and many cabinets, which contain hundreds of small objets d'art, interesting souvenirs and mementos of many journeys and visits. Collections and purchases of works, representing all phases of the industrial arts in which Her Majesty takes so great an interest are here assembled, yet the coloring of the room, with its curtains of blue silk like the walls and a carpet of soft brown bordered with camel color on which is a pale blue rose and green design, brings the floor into harmony with the walls and furniture."

Sadly, as the war continued, there was less time and attention available for fixing up the palace. In fact, the building itself came under attack in October 1915, as Queen Mary noted in her diary: "[A]t 9.30 p.m. they were still sitting in the Palace in G.'s room when we heard a distant report (presumably a bomb) so we went on to the balcony when the gun in Green Park began firing and searchlights were turned on … We did not see the Zeppelin but Derek saw it quite plainly from his house in Buck. Gate. We then heard some bombs being dropped and were told later that some had fallen in the Strand and elsewhere, killing 8 people and injuring 34. All quiet by 10.15."

The east wing of Buckingham Palace in the 1910s

The palace was spared that time, but Buckingham Palace would have less luck a few decades later as the nation once again lurched towards war with Germany. During World War II, the young princesses, Elizabeth and Margaret, were determined to do their part for the war effort. Living at the time in Buckingham Palace, they led the way in founding a Girl Guide Troop that met in the palace each week. Their aunt, Princess Mary, agreed to sponsor the troop and act as its leader.

The 1st Buckingham Palace Company counted among its members 20 Guides, including Princess Elizabeth, and 14 Brownies, including Princess Margaret. The other members were made up of other daughters of the royal household and even members of the palace staff. The king and queen gave the girls the use of a summerhouse for the headquarters, and in the years that followed, the young ladies were often seen pitching tents and cooking over open fires in the palace's extensive gardens. One press report told readers, "At present, the chief hobby of Elizabeth and Margarget, too, is Girl Guides. Both recently passed the tenderfoot tests and early this month their aunt, the Princess Royal, as president of the Girl Guides, will enroll them as 'guide' and 'brownie' respectively. With a group of young friends, children of neighbors when they lived in Piccadilly, they formed the 'First Buckingham Palace Company.' She is studying hard to pass the tests for patrol leader."

Elizabeth during the war

In the end, the girls lost their summerhouse at the beginning of World War II and had to move their activities to the more rural grounds of Windsor Castle. In fact, Buckingham Palace remained a German target throughout the war and was bombed on several occasions, particularly during the Battle of Britain. On September 11, 1940, the king wrote to his mother, "You will have heard about the time bomb which fell near the Garden Entrance at Buckingham Palace last Sunday night, & which exploded on Monday night. I am sending you photographs taken on Monday & Tuesday before & after the explosion showing the damage done…Except for damaging the swimming pool, the main structure of the Palace is untouched. All the windows on each floor were broken. The blast was all upward & only one ceiling is damaged. We were down here at Windsor luckily, & no one in B.P. felt the worse for the 'thud' as the bomb fell on Sunday night, though all our shelters are on that side. Everybody was evacuated on Monday night to the other side of the Palace, in case it exploded & it did at 1.25 a.m."

The official report read in part, "Time bomb has smashed many windows. Some of the ceiling in the Queen's small Chinese room is down. Some damage in Empire Room. The Queen's bedroom and boudoir comparatively undamaged apart from windows. Glass skylight over Minister's staircase is down. Swimming pool extensively damaged at end. Crater 15 ft wide where explosion occurred. No-one hurt. Great quantities of broken glass everywhere on that side of the Palace."

Another attack came days later on September 19, and the queen wrote to her mother-in-law about that one, which would end up being the worst attack the palace sustained: "[W]e heard the unmistakable whirr-whirr of a German plane…there was the noise of aircraft diving at great speed, and then the scream of a bomb. It all happened so quickly that we had only time to look foolishly at each other when the scream hurtled past us and exploded with a tremendous crash in the quadrangle…I saw a great column of smoke & earth thrown up into the air, and then we all dashed like lightening into the corridor. There was another tremendous explosion, and we & our 2 pages…remained for a moment or two in the corridor away from the stair case, in case of flying glass…[Men] were working below the Chapel, and how they survived I don't know. Their whole work-shop was a shambles, for the bomb had gone bang through the floor above them. … I went along to the kitchen which…has a glass roof. I found the chef bustling about…. He was perfectly unmoved…."

In his record of the incident, the king described it as "a ghastly experience yesterday & it was so very unexpected coming as it did out of low clouds & pouring rain at the time. We had just arrived at B.P. from here, & were still in our rooms upstairs. Elizabeth, Alec Hardinge & I were talking in my little room overlooking the quadrangle when it happened. We heard the aircraft, saw the 2 bombs, & then came the resounding crashes in the courtyard. Our windows were open, & nothing in the room moved. We were out of that room & into the passage at once, but we felt none the worse & thanked God that we were still alive…The door opposite the King's Door did not come down. All the windows windows were broken in the passage & the 2 full length pictures of the Duke & Duchess of Cambridge were perforated. But none of the others of the procession. The aircraft was seen flying along the Mall before dropping the bombs. The 2 delay action bombs in front of the Palace have exploded & part of the railings & centre gates are damaged…There is no damage to the Palace itself I am glad to say & no windows are broken. What a good thing it is that the Palace is so thin though & that the bombs fell in the open spaces. It was most certainly a direct attack on B.P. to demolish it, & it won't make me like Hitler any better for it."

The king and queen soon faced an awkward situation in figuring out how to entertain dignitaries in a severely damaged palace. In 1942, First Lady Eleanor Roosevelt visited England on a goodwill mission, and to help coordinate America's support for the British people. Queen Mary wrote to her mother, "It is so dreary at Buckingham Palace, so dirty & dark and draughty, & I long to see the old house tidy & clean once again, with carpets & curtains & no beastly air raids. I feel so sorry for poor Mrs. Ferguson & the housemaids, for it is most depressing having to look after a house that is half ruined! I am putting Mrs. R in my own bedroom upstairs. I have had some small windows put in, and she can use Bertie's own sitting room as mine is dismantled & windowless. It is quite a problem to put up one guest nowadays! She is only bringing a Secretary with her, & travels very simply & quietly."

The queen need not have worried, for though Mrs. Roosevelt had lived her entire life in wealth and privilege, she had still never experienced anything like Buckingham Palace, even in its damaged state. She recalled, "I had been a bit taken aback when I arrived at Buckingham Palace on that trip and was shown my dressing-room with huge closets all around the walls. The maid who unpacked my luggage was well trained but I could see that she was surprised when all she could find to hang up in the enormous expanse of wardrobes was one evening dress, one afternoon dress, a few blouses and an extra skirt!"

Even after the war was over, it still took years for the palace to be restored to its pre-war glory. The young princesses' governess, affectionately called "Crawfie," later wrote, "On wet days when we could not get out, Margaret would say, 'Let's explore.' Then we would wander off round the Palace, to the war-scarred and shut-off apartments where the workmen were busy. During the war the glass chandeliers had all been removed for safety, the pictures and ornaments packed away. Now they were back, waiting to be unpacked and returned to their places, and sometimes we took a hand. It was fun undoing the beautiful crystal pieces and china figures. There was no saying what we might find next. We polished with our handkerchiefs the bits we unpacked…And one day, pottering through the half-dismantled rooms, we came upon a very old piano. Margaret was delighted with this find. She dragged up a packing-case, sat down and proceeded to play Chopin. As she touched the notes, great clouds of dust flew out."

One of the biggest questions was what to do with the chapel that Queen Victoria put in after it had been bombed beyond repair. Finally, the decision was made to rebuild the "exterior without alteration, removing Pennethorne's defacements and restoring the original work of Nash. Pennethorne introduced height by raising the roof but instead of doing this the nave floor has been lowered so as not to interfere with the roof line as originally designed."

The work proceeded according to plan, but there was much more to be concerned about than simply a Victorian chapel. In 1947, Parliament received a report with a cost estimate: "The special work now in hand at Buckingham Palace includes bomb damage repairs, excavation work for a new boiler house and mains in connection with the modernization of the heating system, and the improvement of the servants' quarters in the attics. There is also some work in connection with redecoration of certain rooms and the re-wiring of part of the State rooms. The total cost of this work is about £54,300, of which about half is on bomb damage repairs…The number of men employed is 178. I am satisfied that this work is necessary. The general program for modernizing engineering services in the Palace will be spread over many years, but the opportunity has been taken of the absence of the Royal Family in South Africa to carry out certain noisy and dirty work connected with the installation of new boilers which will be oil fired."

Fortunately, the recovery moved on, and by the time Princess Elizabeth returned to the palace in 1947 with her new husband, the building was looking much better. They only lived there a few months before moving to what they hoped would be their permanent home at Clarence House, but Elizabeth returned to Buckingham Palace as queen just a few years later after losing her father, King George VI, in February 1952. It was difficult for her and Prince Philip to give up the cozy home they had created at Clarence House and move into the drafty palace, in spite of the fact that the new queen had already lived much of her life there. However, as duty always came first for the royals, back to Buckingham Palace they went, with the young prince and princess with them.

In the years that followed, Buckingham Palace continued to see its fair share of births and deaths, marriages, and, new to the later 20th century, divorces. In 1967, Prince Edward, Queen Elizabeth's youngest child, became the last baby to be born in the palace, the modern royals preferring hospital births. It is hard, and somewhat inappropriate, to speculate over if and when Buckingham Palace will be the site of another death for the Royal Family, but there will always be marriages to celebrate in the future. In July 1981, Prince Charles and his bride, Diana, made history and set a new precedent by being the first royal couple to kiss on the balcony, and it is now a much adored tradition. Unfortunately, Charles later became the first heir to the throne to divorce, and then later remarry. Today, he and his wife, the Duchess of Cornwall, live on a country estate and not at Buckingham Palace.

The coming of the 21st century has seen that palace modified and updated to keep current with the latest in technology. Cables run through the ancient walls and satellite dishes are placed discreetly on the roof, with care being taken to do nothing that would diminish the grandeur of the storied residence. The palace remains a large bow that ties the past and the present together, as author Edna Healy so aptly put it: "In 1995, on the fiftieth anniversary of VE Day, the victory in Europe, once again thousands thronged the Mall to cheer The Queen, Prince Philip and the royal family as they made their traditional appearance. As wartime songs rang across the Park, there were many who remembered the courage of King George VI and Queen Elizabeth, who had braved the bombs with the people of London. Viewers caught the unforgettable moment when Queen Elizabeth The Queen Mother, then ninety-five, gave her characteristic wave as she sang with the crowds the wartime song Wish me luck as you wave me goodbye'."

Prince William and President Barack Obama in the 1844 Room in Buckingham Palace

Brendan and Ruth McCartney's aerial photo of Buckingham Palace in the 21st century

Big Ben

DS Pugh's Picture of Big Ben

The bell, which is actually what "Big Ben" refers to, weighs in at 13 tonnes and is 2.28 meters tall and 2.75 meters wide. When the bell was cast, it took more than ten days to cool. The bell was carried on a wagon by sixteen white horses, through roads lined with people eager to see the historic trip.

Big Ben is not the first bell to ring out on the hour at Westminster. Great Tom tolled out the time in the old clock tower starting in 1289. The Palace of Westminster was already an important part of the English parliamentary system by that point. The story of the great clock tower actually starts well before it was built.

Officially the clock was named after Queen Victoria. It was the Victorian Era after all and nearly everything was named after the queen in those days. Each clock dial bears the Latin inscription "Domine Salvam Fac Reginam Nostram Victoriam Primam" which translates to "O

Lord, save our Queen Victoria the First." Considering the tower was just renamed in honor of the current queen, it seems like not much has changed in the last 156 years. It was the people of London, and their love of nicknames that brought on the moniker that most people erroneously believe refers to the tower. As for which Ben is Big Ben named after, that will be discussed in detail further below.

Queen Victoria

The Palace of Westminster

There is so much history concerning the palace and the tower that it is hard to decide where to start. It has been host to many pivotal moments in English history. So where do you start the story of Westminster?

We could go as far back as King Offa, a Mercian King who granted a charter to build a cathedral, or minster, west of London. It was on a tract of land known as the Isle of Thorney, because of the unruly bramble that grew along the shores. Some historians believe that the history of Westminster starts even before Offa. King Sebert is believed to have built a minster west of London in 616. Whatever the official date, the cathedral was in use right up until 943 AD, when Viking raids forced the monks to abandon their church for their own safety.

Edward the Confessor (centre)

The building of a royal palace on these grounds is believed to be the work of the last Anglo-Saxon King of England, Edward the Confessor. Edward had taken a vow of celibacy and had left no heirs to take his throne. The last fourteen years of Edward's life were dedicated to building Westminster Abbey. This new royal residence would become the epicenter of English political life for nearly 1000 years. After Edward's death in 1066, the Abbey was the site of the coronation of the first Norman king, William the Conqueror.

These may seem far removed from the topic at hand, the Elizabeth Tower and its bell, but it is the importance that has been attached to this palace and its clock that have made it a symbol of London, and of England to the whole world; an importance that stems from the major political events that have occurred under the gaze of the clock tower.

The Palace at Westminster has been the meeting place of the British Parliament since the thirteenth century, and so it is not surprising that there are always some big milestones to celebrate.

1215 – The Magna Carta was signed in 1215 and this document that essentially established the rules for the future British parliamentary system is now 800 years old.[87] One of the most important documents in political history, the Magna Carta is still an important part of the British constitution, and has been highly influential in the development of constitutions from around the World.

1265 – Simon De Montfort's Parliament was one of the most revolutionary political happenings of its day. First of all it was a parliament that was not called by the King, probably because Simon De Montfort the 6th Earl of Leicester was holding King Henry III prisoner at the time. The most revolutionary part about this political gathering was that it included townsmen, and lesser landowners, in addition to the Bishops and Barons who normally attended these sorts of things. De Montfort ruled for the imprisoned King for a short time before being killed at the Battle of Evesham on the 4th of August, 1265. His legacy for the country was parliamentary reform that has had ramifications on legislative proceedings for over 750 years. He created a more egalitarian system that included a voice for the common people, and many of his reforms were honored by King Henry's son, King Edward I.

Great Tom

King Edward I, the villain of the Mel Gibson epic *Braveheart*, was a noted political and military genius. He was eager to extend his royal authority across the British Isles. It could also be said that his punishments were rather medieval, but then again so was he; this movie villain also rooted out corruption in his administration. He imprisoned officials who abused their powers and made judges swear to never take bribes. In fact the only gift you could offer a judge was a breakfast, unless that meal was found to be in excess of a normal breakfast. Edward was named after Edward the Confessor, the last of the Anglo-Saxon kings, and the man who built the royal Palace of Westminster.

It was Edward I who called the Model Parliament. It was a conference that included members of the nobility, clergy, and commoners, assembled for the first time by a king. This may seem like a small step considering that De Montfort had already called such a parliament. However, Edward's choice to maintain the political reform of the rebel, and his continued use of this format led to the development of the House of Commons. It makes a difference when the king

---

[87] http://www.bl.uk/magna-carta/articles/magna-carta-an-introduction (Accessed 11/02/2015).

backs the reforms you have made, just ask Oliver Cromwell. Edward, like his father, engaged in many wars, but unlike his father, did not fight against his own people.

To finance his many ambitious wars and castles, the King called two parliaments a year. He used these councils more than any king before him and many of those who came after him. He was never the hated king that his father was, and it was likely the parliamentary system of his rule that caused the people to support him. He was not a tyrant, as the blockbuster movie portrayed him, although hungry for power, he was a just and fairly enlightened king.[88]

The parliaments were held at Westminster and it may have been the importance attached to this place by these councils that led Edward to build the clock tower. The first bell, much like Big Ben, which was officially named after Queen Victoria, was named after King Edward. Much like the modern bell, the original name never took, and the people of London took to calling it Big Ben.

The clock tower of Edward I was not a chiming clock, as the original clock was struck only on the hour. A chiming clock plays melodies for the quarter and half hour marks as well as the hour. Thus, it would be Edward's grandson Edward III would bring England its first chiming clock; in 1367 the clock tower was replaced by a second clock tower, and this chiming clock was to ring out to the people of London for nearly 400 years.

[88]John Thomas Smith, *Antiquities of Westminster; The Old Palace; St. Stephen's Chapel* (London: T. Bensalem, Bolt Court, 1807)

Edward III

Edward III controlled over a quarter of France at the height of his power. His military success had quieted most of his critics, however crises afflicted the latter part of his reign. His gains in France were eventually whittled down to just the port of Calais and the Black Plague not only took his daughter's life, but it had severe social repercussions that could be felt throughout the kingdom. In 1376 the "Good Parliament" went after the king and his advisers and the king went to live out the rest of his days in Windsor. The once great king died at Sheen Palace, Surrey in 1377.

The 1367 renovation, much like the construction took place during a period of parliamentary strength. Edward I and Edward III had needed to maintain support for their expensive wars. These Kings used the machinery of government to accrue both money and political support for their policies. It was these two kings who understood the importance of parliament that built and maintained the clock tower. These kings were able to extend the power and glory of the English throne and levy enormous sums of money from the English people because they understood the importance of the parliamentary system. However, by 1707 the tower had started to crumble.

In 1707, during the reign of Queen Anne, the union of two great nations was at the forefront of the political agenda and not fixing an old clock tower. On May 1, 1707 England and Scotland became Great Britain. That same year the great tower was taken down. The structure was replaced by a sundial. The bell, Great Tom was sent to St. Paul's and there would be no bells ringing in Westminster for the next 150 years.

Queen Anne

The Fire

For a complete hour by hour breakdown of the event one should read Caroline Shenton's _The Day Parliament Burned Down_, published by the Oxford University Press. The official inquest into the causes for the fire and the very public nature of the disaster leant itself very well to this lively and interesting account of the events.

The destruction of both HOUSES of PARLIAMENT by fire Oct 16. 1834

An Illustration of the Destruction of Parliament

By 1834 the Palace of Westminster had been in operation for nearly 800 years. It was one of the most expensive public properties to maintain in Britain. Members of both houses had been complaining about the conditions in the parliamentary palace since the 1790s. The buildings were cramped and permitted very little air flow. In hindsight the fire seems like the perfect solution. However, contemporaries, especially among the commoners of London, felt was that this great fire was a judgment from God. The parliament had just passed the Poor Law Amendment Act of 1834, the subject of Charles Dickens' *Oliver Twist*. There was also the Great Reform Act of 1832, which many believed was pushing democratization too far. Whatever they believed about the fire, many spectators came out to watch parliament burn.

On October 16, 1834, two cartloads of tally sticks were burned in the heating furnaces under the House of Lords. The tally sticks were a medieval holdover used by the Chancellor of the Exchequer as tax receipts. While these sticks were left to burn, a chimney fire started, and would slowly move through the building. It was not until later that evening when the flames were noticed. Confusion set in and the groundskeepers and attendants did not raise the alarm right away. By the time the fire brigades arrived on the scene, it was too late.[89]

It took five days for the fires to completely settle down. The fire brigades were amateur associations in those days, and they were paid in beer. As the fires raged, everyone from MPs to noblemen participated in the firefighting efforts. These efforts were led by Superintendent James

---

[89] M. H. Port, *The Palace of Westminster Surveyed on the Eve of the Conflagration, 1834*, London Topographical Society Publication 171 (2011), 23.

Braidwood, dubbed by many as the "grandfather of modern firefighting theory."[90] The blaze was contained to the palace by the strong stone walls built by the Norman kings 700 years before. In the end Westminster Hall, and parts of St. Mary's Chapel and the Cloister, are the only sections of the old castle that remain to this day.

When the smoke had finally cleared and the rubble had been cleared away, no criminal charges were ever laid. The cause of the fire was determined to be stupidity and error. Then Prime Minister, 2nd Viscount Melbourne stated that the fire had been, "one of the greatest instances of stupidity upon record."[91]

The Making of Big Ben

Big Ben is more than just a bell in a clock tower. It is a cultural icon. Such a building is far more important than any of its component parts. The importance of this structure is cultural, political, and architectural all at once. The rebuilding of Westminster had everything necessary for the creation of myth and legend. There was drama, there was plotting, and there was scandal. When the fire ripped through and destroyed the palace, it was considered by many to be a great loss to the country. So was the rebuild seen as a show of strength, and the designers, and builders, working on the project understood the importance of the work that they undertook.

The Competition

Edward Wedlake Brayley and John Britton in their history of the palace, written just after the fire, describe the efforts to rebuild the Palace as: "The subject is important and national - it belongs to the whole kingdom, and the whole kingdom will be interested, and in some measure implicated, in the honour or disgrace which may become characteristic of the new erections."[92] This book, *The History of the Ancient Palace and Late Houses of Parliament at Westminster,* catalogues the full history and important role that the palace had played in the history of British democracy. The tone of lament is present in this work, and yet one can also surmise the excitement present in London during that period. The competition to win the contract for rebuilding the palace was already under way.

In 1835 a Royal Commission had already decided that the style of the new castle should be Gothic, or Elizabethan. The old palace layout had been rejected. The new castle needed to incorporate the remaining structures, but was not to be a simple rebuilding of the old palace. The next year the competition began. Ninety-seven applicants put forth their proposals with these stipulations in place. The referees unanimously choose entrant 64, the design created by Sir Charles Barry as the winner. With the help of Augustus Welby Northmore Pugin, Barry had

---

[90] Caroline Shenton, "The Fire of 1834" (http://www.historyofparliamentonline.org/periods/modern/fire-1834 accessed 11/2/2015).
[91] Ibid.
[92] Edward Wedlake Bayley and John Britton, *The History of the Ancient Palace and Late Houses of Parliament at Westminster* (London: John Weale, 1836)

created a neo-gothic masterpiece. These two men were leading figures in a revolution in British architecture. Gothic style buildings were popping up everywhere in the Victorian period.

The winning design did not actually include a clock tower. The clock tower was added to the plans later in the year. The clock tower, the face, and the dials were largely the work of A.W.N. Pugin who also designed the clock tower of the Scottish parliament buildings. Neither Pugin nor Barry would live to see the completion of the palace, but it was their vision that made the palace the marvel that remains for us today.

Construction

For four years after winning the contract, Barry and Pugin labored over their plans. In 1840 construction started on the main palace. Three years later construction began on the tower. Public works projects never seem to run on time. That is just a fact, but this project seemed to drag on forever. Not only did the architects not live to see it, but the construction outlasted the Right Honourable 2nd Viscount William Lamb Melbourne who had been elected Prime Minister three times starting in 1834. The construction also outlasted Sir Benjamin Hall, and Big Ben Caunt, the two men of which one is supposed to be the inspiration behind the great bell's nickname.

The gothic style of the outer building was to be continued on the inside as well. In this pursuit Pugin was given a great deal of leniency. As Head of Woodcarving for the project, he was responsible for overseeing the designs of the inside of the building.[93] Every detail and flourish was designed to continue the neo-gothic theme. However the designers also kept in mind the needs of a modern parliament. The buildings were designed to accommodate the legislative bodies that were only growing in importance during the Victorian period.

The palace was rebuilt entirely from sand-colored limestone taken out of the Anston Quarry in Yorkshire. Most of the materials used in the building were from British sources. It was a building of national interest and national materials. The old castle had been built in a piecework style over the course of many centuries. The old palace had much lower walls, and far fewer turrets. The new palace, almost from the very beginnings of the rebuild had captured the imagination of the country. Town halls, churches, schools, and many other public buildings in England and throughout the world were inspired by this building.[94]

The Parliamentary clock tower was built without scaffolding. The construction crews worked from the inside and moved out.

Building the clock inside the tower cost 2500 British Pounds in 1853 or 300,000 by

---

[93] https://www.architecture.com/Explore/Architects/CharlesBarry.aspx (accessed 11/24/15).

[94] http://www.parliament.uk/about/living-heritage/building/palace/architecture/palacestructure/the-stonework/ (accessed 11/02/2015).

today's pound sterling. This may seem like a lot, but it is actually considerably less than the current estimates for the necessary repairs the clock currently needs.[95] It is also surprising when one considers what a feat the clock was technologically. It was the most accurate clock in the world at the time of its unveiling and for a long time afterwards it remained the most scientifically sound public clock standing.

The Issue of Accuracy

The job of designing the clock had originally been given to the Royal Clockmaker, Benjamin Lewis Vulliamy. However, other clockmakers in England believed that they were entitled to throw their hats in the ring as well. One such clockmaker was Edward Dent, a London clockmaker who knew of the prestige one could gain by designing such a clock. Dent pushed so hard for his chance that Sir Charles Barry decided to open up a competition to see who could put forth the best clock design. This was extremely fitting as a similar competition had been used to determine that Barry should design the new palace.

Benjamin Lewis Vulliamy

The Royal Astronomer Sir George Airy was chosen to officiate the contest. Airy set down fairly controversial rules for the construction of the clock that upset many of the hopeful designers. Airy was demanding a clock that was far beyond the accuracy levels of most of the clocks of the day. The most important requirement was that: "The Great Clock should be so

---

[95] http://www.thestar.com/news/insight/2015/11/14/fixing-big-ben-a-towering-task.html (accessed 11/12/15).

accurate that the first strike for each hour shall be accurate to within one second of time."[96] Not only was this very difficult to achieve, but the results would be telegraphed to the Greenwich Observatory twice to ensure that the clock was running properly.[97] This was a daunting task in the mid-nineteenth century.

The fact that it had four faces was itself a challenge. The fact that the faces were 7 meters or 23 feet in diameter did not help much either. The hour hands are each 2.7 meters long and weigh 300 kilograms, and the minute hands are 4.2 meters long and weigh 100 kilograms.[98] This was the largest public clock of its day. A. W.N. Pugin, the designer of the clock faces, had created a stunningly attractive clock, but it would never matter without the mechanisms to run it.

Numerous professional clockmakers submitted their designs for the clock. Vulliamy and Dent were seen as front runners. In the end however, not one of the clockmakers could design a clock that met with Airy's specifications.

Edmund Denison was an amateur clockmaker brought in to help with the judging of the contest. It was his design that was eventually chosen as the winning design. While this hardly seems fair, and must have been seen by some people as a breach of ethics, Denison's clock has been keeping London running for over 150 years,[99] although it was not his first design.

The clock that was originally built from Denison's winning entry was too big for the large tower to hold in its belfry. It would take some modifications in order to get the clock running the way it was designed to in the space available in the clock tower.

It also seemed very unnecessary given the time period. There was no public outcry for a more accurate public clock in London. Most people could not even read a clock at this time. The drive for a superior clock seems to have been motivated by the egos of those people in charge of its design. From the outset of this project there had been a tendency to make the new Palace of Westminster a crowning achievement for the Victorian age.

It was this drive that made the clock tower the landmark that it is today. This stunning achievement in accuracy has made Big Ben synonymous with time in England. The time signal on BBC Radio 4, the opening of the 10 o'clock news on ITV, the big clock and its trademark tone appear on British TV almost every time the issue of "time" is brought up.[100]

The clock was designed to be wound by water or by hand. To wind the clock by hand would take six hours and as one tour guide was heard to remark in 1900, "That is a task unfit even for convicts."[101] The water winding process that is used keeps the clock running smoothly,

[96] Martin Latham, *Londonopolis: A Curious and Quirky History of London* (London: Batsford, 2014), 97.
[97] Ibid.
[98] http://www.englandforever.org/england-big-ben.php (accessed 11/24/15).
[99] Ibid.
[100] MacDonald, *Big Ben*, 5.

but it is nice to know that there is a backup plan in place.

Big Ben Causes Delays

While the clock was extremely accurate, the projections for the completion were well off. The entire palace rebuild was delayed at almost every stage. The rebuild began in 1840 and was projected to last six years. While most of the work was finished two decades later in 1860, there were still parts of the palace under construction until around 1870. It was once again the drive to make this palace a true achievement that caused the delays, and considering the results, it is hard to find fault.

The construction of the Elizabeth Tower was held up for five years because of numerous disputes over supplies and design. The building of the clock was delayed for seven years as the referee for the clock building contract set very high standards for the clock that was to be constructed. As the head of the Greenwich Observatory, Airy had a predisposition toward accuracy and the clock he wanted was going to be the most precise clock the world had yet to see. The striking of each hour was to be within a second of the clock's movements.[102] However, when you look at the complexities of building such a clock, the reasons for the delay become clear. The clockmakers and builders were attempting a clock tower on a scale never before seen on this planet.

The bell itself presented a challenge as the first great bell cracked in the courtyard at Westminster Palace during the testing phase. The foundry that built the bell blamed the clockmaker, Edmund Beckett Denison, for his decision to nearly double the size of the hammer used to ring the bell. Denison saw this as an attempt to remove him from his position of power.[103] However, if you read his book about clock making, he literally thought that about everything that went wrong during the clock project. A new bell was forged and that bell cracked as well. Sir George Airy had the bell turned and adjusted the angle at which the bell was struck by the hammer. The second bell is the one that we now know as Big Ben and it has continued to ring despite the crack for the last 150 plus years.

The clock and the bell were larger than any other clock and bell pairing in the world. It was a completely unprecedented situation. There had been clock towers in the past, but never had they been this large or accurate. Figuring out the mechanics and how to get the bell to ring properly took so long that there has never been an official opening ceremony for Big Ben. The clock started running in 1859, but used one of the quarter hour bells to ring the hour until 1863 when

---

[101] "A CLIMB UP THE CLOCK TOWER AT WESTMINSTER," *The Leisure Hour: A Family Journal of Instruction and Recreation* (Jan. 21 1858), 47.

[102] Randall F. Barron and Brian R. Barron, *Design for Thermal Stresses* (Hoboken, NJ: Wiley & Sons Inc., 2012), 230.

[103] Lord Grimthorpe, *A Rudimentary Treatise on Clocks, Watches and Bells* (London: Virtue & Co., 1868), 189.

Airy found a solution to the cracked bell problem.

The clock tower is possibly the most iconic feature in England. It appears in countless TV shows and movies and has also been a prominent figure in literature. It could be argued that it was worth all the hassle. It is also worthwhile to note that work on the tower was essentially done in 1863, and yet the work continued in the rest of the palace for another seven years as workers continued to bring Barry's vision to life.

Which Ben Was It?

This is a question that modern Londoners still argue over. Is Big Ben, a bell officially named after Queen Victoria, named after the boxer or the parliamentarian?

The case for Ben Caunt seems very strong. The 18 stone (114Kg) boxer and bar owner was a much loved figure in London. His passing coincides with the start of Big Ben as an operational clock.[104] It makes sense that the people of London would name the bell, which was already becoming a staple of life in London, after the beloved athlete. What was the nickname of this prize fighter you may ask?

Benjamin "Big Ben" Caunt's biggest fight was on April 3, 1838 when he went 75 rounds with William Thompson, who fought under the name Bendigo.[105] The match lasted one hour and twenty minutes with Caunt dominating his smaller opponent the whole way. While this theory for the name of the bell seems sound, it should be noted that Caunt was never the heavyweight champion of England. He was popular, but he was not the most popular boxer in London.

The parliamentarian in question is Sir Benjamin Hall. He was the Member of Parliament and Privy Councillor during a long political career that lasted from 1826 until his death in 1867. He was the First Commissioner of Works and Public Buildings during the late stages of the rebuilding of the Palace of Westminster.[106] Was this fact enough for the people of London? Lord John Manners held the same post, First Commissioner of the Works, twice during the rebuild, but we don't call it Big John.

We will likely never know why the bell was given its nickname. The fact is that the bell has become a much more important figure in London, and English culture than either of the Bens it may have been named after.

Heard Throughout the Dominions

During the Second World War, Sir W. Davison, an MP and fervent patriot, believed that

---

[104] Edgar James, *The Lives and Battles of the Champions of England* (Self Published: 1879), 33.

[105] Peter Macdonald, *Big Ben: The Bell, the Clock and the Tower* (London: The History Press, 2013), 100.
[106] Ibid, 101.

people across the British Empire needed inspiration to help them through these dark times. It was the tone of Big Ben that he believed that they needed to hear. Sir Davison presented his idea to the Prime Minister like this:

> In view of the power of concentrated thought, he will consider the desirability of making a broadcast statement, suggesting to British citizens throughout the world that they should as far as possible unite together every night during the minute set aside for reflection at the striking of nine o'clock by Big Ben on some such thought as the continual virility of the British Empire, and how essential is its maintenance for the future peace and freedom of the world.[107]

This minute of reflection was debated in the British Parliament for many months. Some believed that it was impossible because of the varied time zones that the British subjects lived in. This was not a case of British subjectivism, as most of the people in the former colonies considered themselves British citizens. During this time most of the Dominions used British Passports; the Dominion of Canada didn't adopt its red, maple leaf flag until 1967. However, the problem of time zones remained.

The problem was eventually solved by the legislature of New Zealand, which played a recording of Big Ben striking 9 pm at 9 pm local time.[108] It may seem like a simple solution, but this problem was literally debated from February of 1941 until New Zealand resolved it in August of that same year. If it wasn't for New Zealand, they might still be debating this point. Luckily, they did, and the people of the British Empire were able to collectively think about the "Virility" of their Empire.

Davison and his colleagues were excited by the news and pushed to have the practice adopted by the rest of the Dominions. The "Big Ben Minute" as it was dubbed became a cultural touchstone for people experiencing the horrors of total war at home throughout the Empire. The whole experience brought the people of the British Empire closer, and it cemented Big Ben's place in the popular imagination.

The Makers

It is time to get to know some of the key people in the making of Big Ben. I have entitled this section "The Makers" because it is not only about the architects, but also the politicians and the judges who made this vision a reality.

Sir Charles Barry

Barry was born only a stone's throw from his crowning achievement on May 23, 1795. His

---

[107] Great Britain, *House of Commons Hansard*, (02/26/1941).
[108] Great Britain, *House of Commons Hansard*, (08/07/1941).

family lived on Bridge Street, Westminster. He was raised in a middle class family and educated at the finest schools. A statue bearing his likeness was placed inside the walls of Westminster Palace soon after his death, which occurred on May 12, 1860.[109] He left behind five sons and two daughters, many of whom carried on the family interest in architecture. It was his son, E. M. Barry, who oversaw the completion of the New Westminster Palace project. He was laid to rest in Westminster Abbey, just across the street from the palace he designed.

Sir Charles Barry

While he attended the finest schools, many attribute his architectural influences to his many travels throughout Europe and the Middle East. France, Italy, Greece, Turkey, then Egypt, Palestine, Jerusalem, Syria, Damascus, then Cyprus, Rhodes, Halicarnassus, and Malta were all stops for the young Barry.[110] Sicily was a very important trip for the developing architect. It was here that he met John Lewis Wolfe an architect and lifelong friend who had a deep influence on the future work of the new palace designer.[111] Wolfe would eventually leave architecture as a profession, but Barry consulted with his friend when he needed an honest opinion.

In Athens Barry met Mr. D. Baile who admired his drawings and paid him to travel through Egypt. They went through Egypt sketching different buildings and when Baile died, the

[109] Prunella Fraser, Sir Charles Barry (London: Royal Institute of British Architects, 1960), 1.
[110] Ibid, 12.
[111] Ibid.

prints were purchased by his son. The trips to Egypt and Sicily were among the most formative moments of his life. He spent many years travelling around making sketches of old architecture for which he was celebrated upon returning to England.

A member of the Royal Academy of Arts of England, and the academies of St. Luke, Rome, St. Petersburg, Belgium, Prussia, Sweden, and Denmark, Barry was also a member of the American Institute. The Royal Institute of British Architects presented the Queen's Gold Medal for Architecture to him for his work in designing the palace.[112]

Barry got back and competed for small gothic churches which he was successful at, allowing him to marry Miss Sarah Roswell in 1822 after a long engagement, two years after returning from abroad. In 1833 he began King Edward VI's Grammar School at Birmingham and finished in 1836. During that time he met Augustus Pugin and John Thomas who became his "lieutenants" in building parliament. Later, after winning the competition to build Westminster, Barry appointed John Thomas head of stone carving and Pugin head of woodcarving.[113] Sir Charles Barry started his career working in Manchester and became one of the most respected architects in all of the British Isles having built hospitals, libraries, castles, country homes, and churches.

Other Buildings Designed By Sir Charles Barry:

- Holy Trinity Church, Hurstpierpoint.
- All Saints Church, Whitefield.
- The Manchester Art Gallery, Manchester.
- The Royal College of Surgeons of England, Westminster.[114]

Augustus Welby Northmore Pugin

How can you not lead an amazing life with a name like that? A leading voice in the return to Gothic architecture that swept through Britain in the Victorian period, Pugin was highly influential in the designing of Westminster Palace and the Elizabeth Tower. He helped with the drawing of the prize-winning plans in 1835 and worked on the building project off and on until his death at the age of 40.

---

[112] Ibid, 20.
[113] Ibid, 23.
[114] https://en.wikisource.org/wiki/Barry,_Charles_(DNB00) (accessed 11/22/15).

Augustus Welby Northmore Pugin

Like Barry, Pugin travelled Europe as a young man and was inspired by what he saw. At the age of thirteen he went to Paris with his father and started sketching the buildings that caught his eye. People noticed immediately that the boy had a talent for sketching and drawing. He also travelled through Italy, Holland, and Belgium.[115] He assisted his father wife architecture, archaeology and other work.

Pugin was known for his love of the sea even after being shipwrecked off Leith. It was on this same excursion that he met James Gillespie Graham, an architect who helped the young Pugin by offering him a compass. Pugin would later repay the favor by assisting Graham with his sketches for the competition to rebuild Westminster Palace. He was hedging his bets on the contest as he also assisted Barry with his drawings. He is supposed to have said, "There is nothing worth living for but Christian architecture and a boat."[116] While his love of boats seems to have gotten him in trouble, it was his love of Christian, specifically Catholic architecture that was the driving force behind his career.

Pugin converted to Roman Catholicism in 1833 just before marrying his second wife, Louisa

---

[115] Rosemary Hill, God's Architect: Pugin and the Building of Romantic Britain (New York: Penguin Adult, 2008), 13.
[116] Ibid, 24.

Burton. He dreamed of reuniting the churches and he blamed the reformation for what he considered a lowering of the artistic standards of architecture. He hated tobacco and alcohol and wanted to see a return to higher morality. Pugin was married three times but never divorced; he outlived his first two wives. In 1851 Pugin died leaving his third wife to raise his seven children.[117]

A controversial character in London's high society, it is believed that the devout Roman Catholic and moralist's decent into madness and then <u>death</u> was brought on by syphilis. Before he started work on the Westminster project, Pugin had also designed the spire of the <u>Tolbooth Kirk</u>, which among other roles housed the Scottish Parliament until 2004.

Sir George Airy

Born in 1801 in Alnwick, Airy died in 1892 in Greenwich where he worked as the head of the observatory. He was appointed the high honor of Royal Astronomer in 1835 and served the realm in this capacity until 1881.[118] He had already received the hallowed title of Lucasian Professor of Mathematics at Cambridge and the Plumian Professor of Astronomy, also at Cambridge before marrying Richarda Smith in 1830.

---

[117] Ibid, 56.
[118] "George Biddell Airy" http://www-history.mcs.st-and.ac.uk/Biographies/Airy.html (accessed 11/12/15)

Sir George Airy

While very accomplished in the field of astronomy, Sir George Airy is best known for his involvement in the clock design competition that decided who would get the honor of making the clock for the new palace clock tower. He was also famously blamed for allowing the Germans to win the race to find the planet Neptune.[119] However, I am sure he would rather be remembered for the first thing. He was not only the referee of the contest, but he set down the requirements for the clock design. His list of specifications was considered so advanced that many believed designing a clock of this precision and magnitude was an impossible task.

A multitalented man of science, Airy's interests were as varied as calculating the density of the Earth and in Optometry. He was one of the first to use cylindrical glass to treat astigmatism. It was a major breakthrough in the field. He also developed a technique for testing the density of the Earth using pendulums. He would hold them over wells to see the difference in gravity when compared to regular land. He was a leader in several fields of study and so both his appointment as referee and his demands on the designers should have come as no surprise.

---

[119] Ibid.

Lord Grimthorpe, Edmund Beckett Denison

Born on May 12, 1816, Lord Grimthorpe would change his name three times before dying on April 19, 1905 at nearly 90 years old. He was born Edmund Denison and then when he came into his father's Baronetcy, he added his mother's name Beckett. It was later when he became a Baron that he adopted the name 1st Baron Grimthorpe of Grimthorpe, but you could simply call him Lord Grimthorpe. However, that name came after the building of the clock tower. In 1845 Edmund, as Edmund Denison, married Fanny Catherine.

Edmund Beckett, 1st Baron Grimthorpe

Denison was an amateur clockmaker and had only been brought into the clock design competition as an assistant to the referee, Airy. Denison was a Barrister and famous in London court circles for his severe cross examinations. He was not, however, particularly knowledgeable about the law itself. The Baron did enjoy arguing and one of his favorite topics was marriage. Denison wrote four pamphlets dealing with the issue of widowers marrying the sisters of their dead wives.

He was an advocate of the reform in church discipline and was elected president of the Protestant Churchman's Alliance. This was a post that he held with the same fiery passion that he brought to all of his life's pursuits. It makes one wonder about how he got along with the ultra-Catholic Pugin during the building phase. Pugin designed the clock faces and much of the tower itself. The Protestant stalwart Denison would have been very well acquainted with the designer. Denison held very strongly to his convictions and this would be a key factor in many of the holdups that interrupted the clock tower project.

The whole project was one non-stop conflict according to Grimthorpe. He describes the struggle here: "As soon as it was found out that I had any power to effect the work under the contract, every attempt was made to get rid of it and me."[120] The pugnacious lawyer was always looking for a fight. He fought with both foundries over the design of the bell. His struggle to see his vision for the bell come to life lasted seven years. It was only because of his determination that his clock came into existence.

Lord Grimthorpe released a treatise on the making of clocks that many saw as an attack on Sir George Airy's rules for Big Ben. *A Rudimentary Treatise on Clocks, Watches and Bells,* went through ten editions and was the most complete manual on clock making of its day. It is still cited today as an authority on public clocks. The book covers everything from properly laying out a watch face to counteracting gravity escapement when trying to hang your pendulum.

Edward Middleton Barry

Taking over the new palace project on the death of his father, E. M. Barry faced a wave of controversy in his first few years on the job. As the decaying limestone and the numerous delays continued to be key features of Question Period in the British Parliament, the son of Charles Barry was left to defend his father's work. The attacks didn't stop at Parliament. A. W.N. Pugin's son, E. Welby Pugin, declared that it was his father and not Charles Barry who had designed the new palace.[121] Edward's brother, the Reverend A. Barry, took the lead in this fight. Fortunately for the Barry family there were enough associates of their late father left alive to defend his intellectual property.[122] The accusations of Pugin's son were dismissed by London society and the nation at large.

Big Ben in Myth and Legend

The people of London love their giant clock almost as much as they like folklore and urban legend. They pay much attention to their iconic timepiece and any abnormalities are general viewed as omens or signs that occult forces have taken over the running of the city. The clock has predicted the deaths of royals, and the mood of the Irish toward having their own legislature. The clock tower and its bell have a lot to say to those in London who know how to listen.

If He Ever Strikes 13

It is hard to say how any legend begins, but the origins of this tale are especially unclear. The urban legend has been circulating since the 1860s when the big bell finally became fully operational. The myth states that should the great bell ever strike thirteen, the lion sculptures of Trafalgar Square will come to life and no doubt ravage the city and all of England.

---

[120] Lord Grimthorpe, *A Rudimentary Treatise on Clocks, Watches and Bells* (London: Virtue & Co., 1868), 188.
[121] http://www.victorianweb.org/art/architecture/barryem/bio.html (accessed 11/22/15).
[122] Ibid.

A clock striking thirteen times is not an unprecedented event. In fact Big Ben's predecessor Great Tom was said to have rung thirteen times one night when it hung at the Palace. The event was used as evidence by a sentinel at Windsor Palace who stood accused of falling asleep on the job. He would have been sentenced to death if he was found guilty. Several other people had heard the bells being struck that night and the accused was cleared of all charges.

It may seem like a stretch to believe that a simple miscue could bring giant sculpted lions to life, but for at least one Londoner the lucky number thirteen performed miracles. Who's to say that it wouldn't work again?

Emmeline Pankhurst Locked Away

This story was apparently put forward by many reliable sources, but has been recently outed as a hoax. There is in fact a prison cell inside the Elizabeth Tower, but according to records kept at the British Parliamentary Archives it never held the famous suffragette. Pankhurst was apparently accused of opposing parliament and that is why they locked her up, but it was not in the clock tower's cell.

Born into a family known for radical politics, Emmeline Goulden married a lawyer, Richard Pankhurst who was of similar political conviction in 1879. In 1889 she was a founding member of the Women's Franchise League, which wanted to earn the franchise for married women. Later she was also a founding member of the more liberal and even more militant Women's Social and Political Union. This was a group noted for its political stunts and acts of defiance. It was with this group that Emmeline was purportedly locked in the tower.

The story may have been started because it sounds more romantic than being thrown into a normal prison. While she came from a radical family, Emmeline was a respectable woman. However, the prison in the tower, according to most sources is reserved for Members of Parliament who abuse Parliamentary privilege.[123] There is also a report of an MP, Mr. Grissell, who was exiled from England because of money and corruption; the reports implied that he took a bribe for his vote in parliament. His lawyer, Mr. John Ward, was imprisoned in the clock tower.[124] This case from the 1870s features a lawyer being imprisoned, but the issue at stake is the abuse of parliamentary privilege.

Big Ben is Being Controlled by the Occult

In 1905 the color of one of Big Ben's faces changed from red to green and the highly superstitious residents of London did not hesitate to develop their own theories as to why. These rumors and whispers spread like wildfire and the rumblings led to this amazing exchange in the House of Commons on June 29, 1905:

---

[123] http://www.englandforever.org/england-big-ben.php (accessed 11/12/15).
[124] Leigh Hunt, "THE CAPTIVE OF THE CLOCK-TOWER," *Examiner 3730* (July 1879), 952.

Mr. J. F. Hope: I beg to ask the Hon. Member of Lancashire, Chorely, whether he is aware that in the last few days one of the faces of Big Ben has assumed a greenish hue; if so, is he responsible for the phenomenon or is it due to some occult agency?

Lord Balcarres (Lancashire, Chorely): The occult agency is an attempt on the part of the office of works to affect certain economies. The reason why I asked my Hon. Friend to put a notice in the paper, which he has done, is that there are scientific matters involved which I do not understand, and a certain number of foreign words which I am unable to pronounce.

Mr. Hope: Is the noble Lord aware that the phenomenon has been interpreted as an omen that the home rule controversy is entering an acute phase?[125]

The home rule controversy referred to the debate over the need for a legislature in Northern Ireland.[126] In an odd twist, this controversy was about the people not wanting their own government. The Northern Irish actually rioted over the establishment of this nominal self-governing situation. Then in 1914 they rioted again, only this time it was over the fact the British Parliament had added a stipulation to the development of an Irish legislature that said that the Government of Great Britain could override the decisions of the Irish legislature.[127]

As it turned out the green light was an experiment. The green light was being tested for its effectiveness as it would save the government 35% on the 242 pounds that they spent annually on lighting the clock faces of Big Ben.[128] There was an advertisement put in the papers, but it doesn't seem like everyone took notice.

The Bells Predict the End for the Duchess of Kent

The people of London pay very close attention to their great clock tower. In March 14, 1861 there was a misfiring of the mechanisms in the tower and Big Ben rang out ten and twelve tolls at 4 am and 5 am that same morning. People thought that this was done purposefully to announce that a member of the royal family was dead. In the end it was just a defect in the clock. However, that same day it was discovered that the Duchess of Kent who was Queen Victoria's mother was dying. On March 16, two days after the bells tolled, the Queen's mother had died.[129] Coincidence? It is exceedingly likely that it was one, however, it is also kind of weird that it happened.

---

[125] Great Britain, *House of Commons Hansard* (1905).

[126] C.N. Trueman, "Home Rule and Ireland," http://www.historylearningsite.co.uk/ireland-1845-to-1922/home-rule-and-ireland/ (accessed 11/13/15).

[127] Ibid.

[128] Great Britain, *House of Commons Hansard* (1905).

[129] Morton S. Freeman, A New Dictionary of Eponyms (Oxford: Oxford University Press, 2002), 83.

Big Ben is Falling Apart!

On Oct. 19, 2015 CBS News reported that the old clock was in such a state of disrepair that the minute hands may actually fall off. This led to speculation that Big Ben may be shut down in the coming months. The estimates for the repairs are around 40 million British Pounds.[130] It looks as though the days for the great clock are numbered. However, this is not the first time that the tower has been under this kind of duress. In fact, from the beginning, there have been concerns about the tower's well-being.

In the 1860s, before the rebuilding of Westminster was even finished, there was a parliamentary inquisition that looked into the stability of the limestone that the palace had been built with. The Magnesian limestone from the Anston Quarry was already starting to decay. In 1861 the Report of the Committee on the Decay of Stone (New Palace at Westminster) was placed on the desk of the Right Honourable MP William Cowper, who at the time served as Chief Commissioner of the Works, etc. The report included evidence from a number of sources. One of the foremen on the rebuild team claimed to have known that the stone was about to rot and claims to have sent back several blocks of stone that were unsuitable for the palace.[131] There were several chemical processes that were put forward by contractors. The contractors believed that they could stop the decay. However, E.M. Barry, who took over the works from his father Charles, believed that the stones would heal themselves and defended his father's choice of the Anston Quarry stones.[132] The matter was settled and the stones were left untreated.

As the clock ages, the concerns continue to grow. The clock tower is leaning. That seems like a major concern. The process has been very gradual, but with each passing year the top of Big Ben is getting closer to its bottom.[133] There is also a very real concern that the hands on all four of the giant clock faces may fall off the 90 metre tower.[134] That would have to cause problems. Each one weighing at least a ton, I am sure it wouldn't take long for those things to reach breakneck speed on their way down.

It has been 31 years since the last major overhaul was performed on the Elizabeth Tower. The costs for repairs are only going up. There is also a plan to add an elevator for tourists.[135] The British Parliament and the British people for that matter are torn on the subject, but if something is not done soon, it may be too late.

---

[130] http://www.bbc.com/news/uk-england-london-34565724 (accessed 11/23/15).
[131] Great Britain, *Accounts and Papers of the House of Commons vol. XXXV* (1861).
[132] Ibid.
[133] http://www.bbc.com/news/uk-wales-south-east-wales-30623562 (accessed 11/12/15).
[134] http://www.bbc.com/news/uk-england-london-34051053 (accessed 11/12/15).
[135] Ibid.

The Elizabeth Tower, as Photographed by Diego Delso

The clock in the Elizabeth Tower is also having trouble with accuracy lately. You can almost feel George Airy rolling over in his grave as the BBC reports that clocksmith Ian Westworth considers the bell striking within two seconds of the time is on time.[136] This same clocksmith thought that the six second delay Big Ben experienced earlier this year was normal for an old clock. The pendulum for the great clock is now monitored with a system of stacked pennies. The weight of a single penny can affect the motion of the clock by 0.4 seconds per day.[137] It sounds like nothing, but that is a lot of time per year for a public timepiece being acted upon by a penny.

Archaeology at Westminster

The age of the buildings and the important role that the site has played in the history of the nation is a history that includes Viking raids, the Norman Conquest, and over a millennium of service as a royal dwelling and official government building. You know there has to be tons to uncover when there is a 900 year old palace called "New" Palace Yard.

In May of 2015 *The Guardian* reported that archaeology crews would be digging at Westminster Palace for the first time in several years. The team was looking for "Great Tom," the predecessor to Big Ben. This was the original bell from the clock tower that burnt down in 1834.

---

[136] http://www.bbc.com/news/uk-england-london-10950547 (Accessed 11/14/15).
[137] http://www.englandforever.org/england-big-ben.php (accessed 11/14/15).

This may seem confusing as we have already learned about the fate of Great Tom. However, it is possible that they are trying to find the remnants of the old bell tower and not that of the bell. Great Tom was of course recast and now hangs in St. Paul's Cathedral and bears the inscription "Brought from the ruins of Westminster."[138]

However, this expedition is only one of many archaeological queries that have taken place on the palace grounds. This ancient site has been a center for governance and religion for hundreds of years. The very walls of the place are alive with history.

When the Bells Fall Silent

After reading the title, it seems sort of ominous, but that is actually a good thing because the reasons for Big Ben's silence are usually kind of dreary. The clock has fallen silent for repairs. In 1859, only a few months after starting to ring, the big bell cracked. In 1912, there was a problem with the inner mechanisms. In 1934, Members of Parliament were upset at the length of time that the scaffolding had covered the tower and demanded a time frame for restarting the clock from the Commissioner of Works. These are a few of the times that the clock was stopped on purpose.

The bells went silent for the duration of The Great War, or World War I, however you like to describe it. It wasn't until after the Treaty of Versailles was signed in 1918 that the British Parliament entertained the idea of ringing the bells again. The mechanism had broken in 1912 for a period as well, but the repairs were not done until the end of the war.

---

[138] John Timbs, *Curiosities of London*,
https://books.google.ca/books?id=1vw9AAAAcAAJ&pg=PA39&dq=bell,+chime,+Westminster+%22Great+To m%22&hl=en&sa=X&ved=0ahUKEwjAusKQ97nJAhWGeD4KHdboCJwQ6AEIJTAA#v=onepage&q=bell%2 C%20chime%2C%20Westminster%20%20%22Great%20Tom%22&f=false (accessed 11/10/15)

An English Observer during the Battle of Britain

The bells were still chiming when the second "I" was added to the words World War. However, during the Battle of Britain the British Parliament was no longer worried about the cost of lighting the clock faces at night. Air raid regulations forced the clock tower to remain dark throughout the night.[139] Even though it remained dark, many Londoners were left wondering how such a large landmark was left standing through the fury of the German attack. There was some superficial damage that had to be repaired, but the tower stood up to the challenge. While we may never know, a strong case has been made for pure luck.[140]

On April 17, 2013 Big Ben was silenced for the funeral of Lady Margret Thatcher. Known as the "Iron Lady," the first female British Prime Minister was a political force throughout her illustrious career. The bells fell silent as a mark of respect for this much loved figure.[141]

Copycats

If you do anything worthwhile in this world there will be tons of people lined up to imitate you. That is why there are so many towers out there trying to capture just a little bit of that Big Ben magic. There are of course the miniature versions that you can buy at toy stores and souvenir shops all over London. There's also the miniature version of Big Ben in Las Vegas, but they

---

[139] Peter MacDonald, *Big Ben: The Bell, the Clock and the Tower* (London: The History Press, 2013), 236.

[140] http://www.slate.com/blogs/quora/2015/05/25/world_war_ii_why_wasn_t_big_ben_bombed_during_the_blitz.html (accessed 11/23/15).

[141] http://www.theguardian.com/politics/2013/apr/15/margaret-thatcher-big-ben-silenced (accessed 11/21/15).

have miniature versions of everything. This section is just about the most remarkable of the Big Ben copycats.

In 2009 world famous card stacker Bryan Berg was brought to Las Vegas to recreate Big Ben using his artistic medium, cards. It took 600 decks of cards and 40 hours of work, and the finished product was over seven feet tall. The construction of this replica involved no tape, glue, or adhesive measures of any kind. The whole thing was watched over by the Guinness Book of World Records. Mr. Berg was already a record holder at the time. The project lasted six days and as Berg stood up and walked away from his creation, two of his friends walked up to congratulate him and ended up destroying the recreation.[142] There is a video you can watch here.

The Big Ben of Yemen is smaller and made of brick, but from far away it kind of looks like the original. The tower was built in 1890 in Aden, a port city in Yemen. The British controlled the port city at the time and the tower was built by a British company. It is definitely based on its London counterpart. The tower fell into disuse after the town joined independent Yemen in 1960. It was then fixed and ran briefly in 1983. In 2012 the clock tower started to run again and it has become a real landmark for the local population. Currently the locals are worried about the building boom in the area obscuring the landmark. Their Big Ben is somewhat of a highlight for people planning a trip to Aden.[143]

India Today reported in October of 2015 that a 90-ft tall replica of Big Ben has been erected in Kolkata in the hopes of making the town more prosperous. It is believed that the tower will help bring some of that London Financial magic to the Indian city. As to whether or not that is true, I guess only time will tell. Too corny?

Big Ben's Detractors

Nearly the whole world loves Big Ben. There is no way to please everybody, and while there are some people who just plainly don't care about the Queen Elizabeth Tower and its bell, this is a section reserved for people who hate Big Ben.

It starts with Edmund Beckett Denison, the clock designer. He didn't hate the whole thing. His anger was reserved for the bell itself.

I published that Big Ben II was a disgrace to its founders. The workmen asserted that it was impossible to make large bells without holes and that these holes were regularly filled up with cement coloured with bell dust. Sir. G. Airy came and judged the bells to be all out of tune, then changed his mind. He said the crack in Big Ben II was probably superficial and that it would be fine for use. Dr. Percy, the one who investigated the bell,

---

[142] The Telegraph, http://www.telegraph.co.uk/news/newstopics/howaboutthat/5850654/Man-accidentally-destroys-Big-Ben-tower-of-cards.html (accessed 11/08/15)
[143] http://www.bbc.com/news/blogs-news-from-elsewhere-29075673 (accessed 11/13/15).

found it to be very unsound and the crack to be three inches deep.[144]

That was how Denison described his disgust with the bell and also with Airy's decision to use the bell that had been deemed unfit originally. The book that this text comes out of is a very dry and serious text about horology, clock making. However, Denison breaks off in quite a few places to complain about Big Ben, Sir George Airy, and many of the other people involved in the making of the clock tower.

H. R. Haweis says Big Ben is proof the British are not musical people and nothing more exasperating to bell connoisseurs has ever been hung. Big Ben and his four discordant quarters, according to Haweis, teach generations of schoolboys to whistle out of tune. He describes the bell's tone as the "gong-like roar of that brazen fiend."[145] Haweis goes on to compare Big Ben to Dagon, saying his beautiful case might have held a saintly bell instead of "this Dagon and his four discordant satellites." He says he is including this in his piece because the public would be upset otherwise.[146]

Just as a small aside and to help people understand the depth of hatred contained in this passage, I want to take a minute to explain Dagon. Dagon is the half-man, and half-fish god of the Philistines. Worship for this deity began in Eastern Mesopotamia over 5000 years ago.[147] Dagon is mentioned in the Bible. When the Philistines steal the Ark of the Covenant, they take it to the temple of Dagon.[148]

> Haweis believed that the inscription was of the worst, narrow kind. He claimed that the Gothic caricatures had been designed to hide information. The noted clock connoisseur believed that 200 years of dust would render the inscriptions unreadable. He expressed in his book a sincere hope that the bell would be taken down long before then. In his passionate and angry discourse on the subject, Haweis keeps repeating, "The English are a musical people!"[149] One can hear the contempt in his text as he tries to understand how a musical people can be content to listen to a gong. Just to be clear to gong fans out there, Haweis is using the term derogatorily. The English must learn more about music and what to listen for in bells before bell music can be introduced to England.[150]

A Timeline

This timeline was made using the British Parliamentary Website's timeline, which can be found if you follow this footnote.[151]

---

[144] Lord Grimthorpe, *A Rudimentary Treatise on Clocks, Watches and Bells* (London: Virtue & Co., 1868), 191.
[145] H.R. Haweis, "Bells and Belfries," English Illustrated Magazine 77 (1890), 383.
[146] Ibid, 388.
[147] http://www.bible-history.com/past/dagon.html (Accessed 11/12/15).
[148] *Holy Bible*, "1 Sam 5: 2-5,"
[149] Haweis, "Bells and Belfries," 385.
[150] Ibid, 389.

1289-90

Featuring only one dial and a single bell, the first clock tower was erected in the New Palace Yard by King Edward I.

1367

A new clock tower is erected. The new tower chimes the quarter and half hours as well as the hour. This new clock is the first chiming clock in England.

1699

This year signals the end for Great Tom. The original big bell of Parliament is removed and placed in storage. It is eventually sent to St. Paul's Cathedral.

1707

A sundial takes the place of the decrepit old clock tower.

1716

This is the year in which Great Tom is actually recast, because it was dropped on its way out of the bell tower. The bell is hung in St. Paul's. Great Tom rings out when Big Ben is unable to chime.

1834

The palace is almost entirely destroyed by fire. There are parts of St. Stephen's and St. Mary's Chapels that still remain along with the great hall. The fire takes five days to subside.

1840

Charles Barry begins construction on the new palace.

1843

Not added to the designs until after winning the competition, the construction of the clock tower starts three years after the rest of the palace.

1846

London clock makers all want a shot at designing the clock for the palace tower. The competition opens and Sir George Airy, Royal Astronomer is named as the referee, with Edmund Denison appointed as his assistant. Denison also wins the contest.

1852

London Clock maker Edward Dent is award the contract to make Denison's clock, and even though the building will not be finished for nearly twenty years, Queen Victoria declares it open. There is never an official opening for the tower.

---

[151] http://www.parliament.uk/about/living-heritage/building/palace/big-ben/key-dates-/ (accessed 11/12/15).

1854

The clock is finished by Dent's stepson Frederick Dent. This is actually a continuing theme for the rebuilding project.

1856

Warners of Norton cast the first bell officially dubbed the "Royal Victoria." This name however never took off. It was replaced of course by the current nickname.

1857

This first bell cracks during the testing phase. Denison blames the foundry, the foundry blames Denison. The fighting is so ugly that the second bell has to be cast by a different foundry altogether.

1858

Whitechapel Bell Foundry of east London is chosen to cast the second bell. Transported by 16 white horses to New Palace Yard, the bell is cast with several holes that are filled with concrete.

1859

In May the clock starts keeping the time. By July the hour is being struck on Big Ben. A crack develops before the year is out and we are back to square one. A quarter bell is used to strike the hour.

1860

Charles Barry dies. E.M. Barry takes over the rebuild project.

1863

Sir George Airy suggests turning the bell and reducing the size of the hammer. The cracked bell has continued to ring to this day. Denison also blames the second foundry.

1923

This is the first New Year's Eve marked by the broadcasting of Big Ben's chimes on BBC Radio.

1932

BBC Radio airs King George VI's Christmas broadcast and Big Ben's chime is heard internationally for the first time in its history.

1939

Due to air raids, blackout restrictions are put into effect. The dials of the great clock will not shine until victory is declared.

1940

The "Silent Minute" or "Big Ben Minute" is introduced to the British people as a way to keep up morale in war time. It took exactly a minute to broadcast the clock striking 9 o'clock. The debate would range until August of 1941 as MP's debated how to bring this minute of positive thinking to the Dominions.

1945

The lights shine bright again. The air raid bans are lifted when victory is declared and Big Ben is once again illuminated.

1976

In the middle of the night on the 10 August, a mechanical failure caused serious damage to the Great Clock. The pendulum weights fell out of control down the shaft and the clock mechanism exploded. Big Ben was silenced for nearly nine months while repairs were carried out.

2007

Seven weeks of maintenance was put a hold on the ringing of the quarter bells.

2009

Big Ben turns 150 years old and the Nation celebrates the occasion with festivities and events.

2012

The Clock Tower was renamed the Elizabeth Tower to honour Queen Elizabeth's Diamond Jubilee.

Present

You read a book about Big Ben.

In Conclusion

Big Ben is actually the name of the bell. I know it has been a while since I mentioned that fact, but if you remember nothing else…well then, you should probably reread the book. Also you need to remember that the Palace at Westminster was built on what used to be Thorney Island. The land around the island was drained and built upon. This will be important when the tower eventually falls and people ask you why. You can then reply with something akin to what I just wrote above.

The history of Big Ben is more than just the story of a bell. It is the story of people living in close proximity. It is the fireworks on New Year's Eve that shoot out of the top of the tower. It is the countless movies that use an establishing shot of Big Ben to tell the audience that the film takes place in London or is in some way British. It is that iconic tone that was cool way before it became a ring tone. From the very beginning when the crowds flocked to see the bell pulled through the city by 16 white horses, the bell has been a part of the culture of London. Even the first one that never made it into the tower is a part of the lore.

The history of the building is tied directly to the history of British Parliamentary politics. It was the necessity of calling a parliament to raise money that saw the raising of the first clock tower. It was the existence of the first clock tower and the central role that Westminster played in the governance of Britain that made rebuilding the palace and therefore building the new clock tower of such national importance.

It is also important to remember that Big Ben is an impressive part of the London skyline even without all the history. It is one of the most accurate clocks in the world at this time, as well as being one of the largest. The 90 meter tower laughed at the fury of the Luftwaffe during the Battle of Britain. It is a tower that has stood through a lot of history, while creating some of its own.

The Tower Bridge

London Bridge and the Need for Other Bridges

When London was debating the construction of the Tower Bridge in its current spot around the end of the 19th century, it was already well-known that bridges had existed there in the past, but it obviously didn't have the history that London Bridge did. In a lecture given in 1893, civil engineer John Wolfe Berry noted, "A bridge appears to have existed on the site, or a few yards lower down the river than the site, of the present London Bridge, from remote antiquity. We read of Canute attacking and being repulsed from London Bridge, and some writers have held that a bridge at this spot dates from the Roman occupation of London, which was then known to the world as the town Augusta, and must have been of considerable importance…Stow says that in the year 994 the Danes were repulsed in an attack which they made on London, because they took no heed of the bridge; but probably there is some misconception here, for it is recorded that only in the previous year Anlaf, the Dane, sailed up the Thames as far as Staines with ninety-three ships and ravaged the country. Discarding the tradition of a Roman bridge, it seems clear that the first London Bridge of which any record exists was erected between the years 993 and 1016, when Canute attacked London a second time, and made a canal on the south side of the river so as to bring his ships past the bridge."

A medieval depiction of Canute the Great

Berry speculated that the first bridge "was probably of wood…the piers being formed of piles driven into the bed of the river, and the openings spanned by timber beams. … This wooden bridge had great vicissitudes. It was washed away in a flood in 1091, was rebuilt m 1097, and burnt in 1136. It was again rebuilt, but was in so bad a state in 1163 that a new bridge was resolved on, and this time in more durable materials."

It seems that a monk named Peter, then serving as Curate of St. Mary in Colechurch, had at some point in his life trained as a bridge builder. Thus, the Romans hired him to build a new stone bridge near the site, a task that he gave his life to, working on it from 1176-1202. The bridge was finally completed in 1209, but even though stone was obviously sturdier than wood, it was still not permanent, at least not in this case. By 1282, years of freezing and flooding had taken their toll, and large portions of the bridge's support structure had fallen into disrepair.

Instead of replacing the bridge, however, it was repaired and continued to stand for another six centuries. Initially, the bridge's supports were only above 9 feet above the riverbed they were sunk in. As time went only, various builders added more height, including starlings that raised the height of the bridge by another three feet. Perhaps to encourage those who were making pilgrimages, which were treacherous journeys in the Middle Ages, the Chapel of St. Thomas on the Bridge was built at one end of the bridge. This large, rectangular building measured 65 feet long by 20 feet wide but was only about 14 feet tall. Because of its length, it is likely that the chapel extended onto the pier leading to the bridge.

A depiction of the exterior of the chapel

Depictions of the interior

Though it was low, this bridge shared one quality with its descendant in that it had a drawbridge at one end to allow ships to pass through. Of course, this drawbridge was also handy in case of attack, as it could be raised and thus prevent the enemy from using the bridge to cross the river.

Later, in 1426, as England went to war again against France, King Henry VI ordered a tower to be built on the north side of the bridge. This was also a defensive move, as was the decision in 1471 to begin to build small houses on the bridge. This allowed guards to be stationed there permanently for the express purpose of watching for and defending invasion.

Henry VI

Over time, more houses were added, among them Nonsuch House in 1579, one of the most beautiful structures of the time. Writing in *Old and New London, Volume 2*, Walter Thornbury explained, "About the same time was also reared that wonder of London, Nonsuch House—a huge wooden pile, four storeys high, with cupolas and turrets at each corner, brought from

Holland, and erected with wooden pegs instead of nails. It stood over the seventh and eighth arches, on the north side of the drawbridge. There were carved wooden galleries outside the long lines of transom-casements, and the panels between were richly carved and gilt."

Ben Sutherland's picture of a model of Nonsuch House

Three years later, crews of workmen built waterwheels into several of the arches, and they in turn powered a pump to send water into London.

By the early part of the 17th century, there were dozens of homes and other buildings located on what was then known as London Bridge. Then, in 1632, disaster struck when fire broke out and 42 of them were lost. Their owners soon rebuilt, only to be wiped out again during the Great Fire of London in1666. By this time, the bridge itself had become such an important business district that it could not be abandoned and, by the mid-1670s, new buildings had replaced those lost.

In 1725, some industrious soul took it upon himself to measure the bridge and reported it to be 915 feet long and 73 feet wide, with a road only 20 feet wide running across it. It also sat 43 and a half feet above the water. Because of its height, crossing it proved to be quite a chore, especially for anyone pushing a hand cart or carrying a parcel. However, those living on and near it still considered it state of the art, with one poet writing:

"When Neptune from his billows London spyed,

Brought proudly thither by a high Spring-tide,

As through a floating wood he steered along,

And dancing castles clustered in a throng;

When he beheld a mighty bridge give law

Unto his surges and their fury awe;

When such a shelf of cataracts did roar,

As if the Thames with Nile had changed her shore;

When he such massy walls, such towers, did eye,

Such posts, such irons, upon his back to lye;

When such vast arches he observed, that might

Nineteen Rialtos make for depth and height:

When the Cerulean God these things surveyed,

He shook his trident, and astonished said

Let the whole earth now all the wonders count,

This bridge of wonders is the paramount!"

By the mid-18ᵗʰ Century there was enough traffic on the London Bridge to cause regular problems. Therefore, the government decided to tear down most of the houses on it to widen the road and create two footpaths that would themselves be wide enough to facilitate foot traffic. At the same time, those in charge also began to look for other ways in which the bridge could be improved.

Among the designs submitted was one by the famous architect Sir Christopher Wren. While his was one of the few that actually addressed the problem of navigating under the bridge, it was rejected, along with many others. Instead, the center pier supporting the bridge was removed, widening the passage under it to 70 feet.

Sir Christopher Wren

Unfortunately, this proved to be only a temporary fix, and those in charge of the bridge continued to look for new and better solutions. As a result, in 1824, work began on a new bridge, this one designed by John Rennie and completed by his son, Sir John Rennie the Younger. It took seven years to complete and cost 1.5 million pounds. It was beautiful and elegant, but not terribly serviceable, primarily because it was so steep. Making matters worse, it was never enough, to the extent that by the mid-19th century, Parliament had finally recognized the need for an additional way across the Thames.

REMAINS OF THE CHAPEL OF ST. THOMAS, OLD LONDON BRIDGE (*page* 10). *From a View taken during its demolition.*

An 1832 depiction of the demolition of the Chapel of St. Thomas on the Bridge as part of renovations

John Rennie

Sir John Rennie the Younger

Designing the Tower Bridge

Even as Rennie's bridge was being built, the plan for what would become Tower Bridge was in the works. On December 18, 1824, *The Portfolio* published a proposal for an elevated roadway designed by Sea Captain Samuel Brown, with the help of civil engineer James Walker. 1,000 yards long, it was intended to run from east of the Tower moat to a new dock then being built on the original site of St. Katherine's Hospital. Brown, who had made a fortune by inventing a new and better iron chain, had recently completed work on a chain pier in Brighton.

Historian Denise Silvester-Carr described the proposed design: "The engraving in The Portfolio showed the graceful silhouette of an 80ft high bridge suspended on iron chains between four stone piers. Brown produced figures to indicate that tolls would yield 100 [pounds] a day, but nothing came of this much admired undertaking and 'St Katharine's Bridge of Suspension' -- the future Tower Bridge -- was forgotten for almost fifty years."

In 1876, the Metropolitan Board of Works, in charge of transportation systems in the city, asked Parliament for permission to construct a high level bridge. When completed, their creation would stand on the site of the Tower Bridge. Their proposal called for it to be shaped as a single arch supporting 850 feet of bridge 65 feet above the river. A long, straight road would lead to its north entrance, while its southern entrance would form a spiral. The gradient on each would be a gentle "1 in 40," meaning the road would rise one foot for each 40 feet. The board predicted the new bridge would cost about 1.5 million pounds to build, but that this money could be recovered by the tolls placed on crossing.

In spite of the bridge's height, local ship owners still insisted that it would cause problems for large ships plying the river, while those living near the sites of the north and south entrances complained that the approaches, being around a mile long, would disrupt their lives and neighborhoods. As a result, the plan was ultimately rejected.

Then, in December 1876, *Lloyds Weekly London Newspaper* reported, "At Thursday's meeting of the Court of Common Council a report was brought up from the Special Bridge and Subway committee by Mr. H. A. Isaacs, the chairman, recommending that a bridge over or a subway under the Thames should be constructed eastwaid of London-bridge, and that the most eligible site would be that approached from Little Tower-hill and Irongate Stairs on the north side, and from Horsely-down-lane and stairs on the south-side of the river. The discussion upon the report was postponed until after the vacation."

Some days later, the newspaper *Iron* listed the proposals that had been made thus far for the bridge: "They were attended by all the parties, who were severally heard in relation to and explanation of their respective designs and schemes. They also examined the designs submitted to them by…persons which had not been referred to them by the court…The committee further suggested that they should be authorized to advertise for designs and to offer premiums for those most approved. It was agreed to postpone the discussion until after the meeting, the rival report recommending the widening of the existing bridge being also postponed. Among the private Bills in Parliament for the ensuing session deposited on Saturday was one to enable the Corporation of the City of London, the Metropolitan Board of Works and a company, to be incorporated, to build a bridge on the site recommended by the Bridge and Subway Committee appointed by the Corporation of the City…The cost of the bridge, with approaches, is set down as…370,000 [pounds]. The approach on the City side of the river, it is proposed, shall abut on the new street proposed to be made by the Metropolitan Board of Works. The traffic of the new bridge will be as constant and uninterrupted as that of an ordinary public road, and it is announced that the gradients of its approaches, as well as of the bridge itself, are much easier than those of London Bridge."

Much of the money used to finance the construction of the new bridge came from a unique source: the Bridge House Estates Trust. According to its website, "By the end of the 13th century the shops and houses adorning Peter de Colechurch's new stone London Bridge were beginning to generate not only increased cross-river trade, but also increased taxes, rents and bequests. A significant fund began to accumulate and it was administered from a building on the south side of the bridge called Bridge House, with the fund becoming known as the Bridge House Estates…Over the centuries the fund prospered mightily …. The Bridgemasters maximized income from a great variety of sources including…'receiving tolls on carts passing over the Bridge, tolls from ships passing under the Bridge and fines for unlawful fishing from the Bridge'. … In relatively recent years the charity…constructed Tower Bridge."

In addition to monies collected through taxation, the Trust was also gifted through the years with bequests left to "God and the Bridge" by businessmen who had prospered as a result of their location on the bridge. The fund had previously been used to build two other bridges, and now it would finance Tower Bridge.

With that, the committee was given permission to host a public competition to find the best design for the new bridge, but after the search began, it proved to take longer and be more complicated than anyone could have imagined. Writing some years after the bridge was completed, engineer Archibold Williams explained, "Among the many plans submitted since 1867 for a bridge, one is particularly noticeable for its originality — that of Mr. C. Barclay Bruce. He proposed a rolling bridge, to consist of a platform 300 feet long and 100 wide, which should be propelled from shore to shore over rollers placed at the top of a series of piers 100 feet apart. The platform would have a bearing at two points at least, and, according to the designer's calculations, make the journey in three minutes, with a freight of 100 vehicles and 1400 passengers…Another engineer, Mr. F. T. Palmer, proposed a bridge which widened out into a circular form near each shore, enclosing a space into which a vessel might pass by the removal of one side on rollers while traffic continued on the other side. As soon as the vessel had entered the enclosure the sliding platform would be closed again, and that on the other side be opened in turn."

Among those who submitted sketches was Sir Joseph Bazalgette, already known for having designed a number of bridges in and around London, including Maidstone Bridge in 1879. Williams noted that "Bazalgette, engineer to the Metropolitan Board of Works, recommended the construction of a bridge that should give a clear headway of 65 feet above Trinity high-water level, but a Bill brought into Parliament for power to build it was thrown out on the ground that the headway would be insufficient, and on account of the awkward special approaches."

Bazalgette

In spite of his experience, Bazalgette ultimately lost out on his bid to Sir Horace Jones, London's City Architect at the time and, in a blatant example of conflict of interest, one of the judges of the competition. Historian Denise Silvester-Carr observed, "Whether Jones had seen Captain Brown's proposal is not known but in 1878 he suggested that chains should be used to raise the road on a crossing designed to resemble a medieval drawbridge. Twin turrets were deliberately intended to look like the corners of the White Tower at the Tower of London. But the curved steel span would not give sufficient clearance for the bascules…to open fully, and Jones temporarily shelved his 'hasty' plan…Six years later, when a select committee of the House of Commons was discussing the Thames bridges, Jones resurrected the bascule bridge. With the assistance of Sir John Wolfe Barry, the engineer son of the architect of the Houses of Parliament, he submitted a modified scheme. A straight span which would act as a high level walkway was substituted for the arch; hydraulic machinery instead of chains would raise two bascules; lifts would carry passengers up to the walkways and prevent undue delay when ships were passing through."

Jones

Barry

In fact, Jones himself described his bridge as follows: "Apart from the question of appearance and convenience in the passage of vessels, it will render the construction of our road and approaches lighter than in the former bridges, as we should be able to obtain a gradient of 1 in 40 on the south side to the centre of the present level in Tooley Street without any interference with the present level of that street; this would of course give a considerable saving both in compensation and in work. …the waterway would be obstructed by two piers only of, say, 40 feet each, leaving between them a clear way of 200 feet in the centre; the waterway would therefore be 800 feet at high water mark…foot traffic need not be interrupted even when the bridge is open for the passage of vessels staircases must be constructed for the service of the bridge, and they can, as well as passenger lifts, be so constructed as to serve the public. The convenience to the occupiers or riparian owners, east or west, having nothing before them to interfere with the approach to their wharves, will be an additional advantage, and small craft could pass underneath with greater safety and convenience…."

In October 1884, Barry wrote to Jones, "I have given the subject of the Tower Bridge as much consideration as the time which has been at my disposal since you did me the honour of consulting me would allow. … With respect to the opening portion of the bridge, I would recommend that the fairway between the tiers of shipping should be kept clear when the bridge is open, and that no centre pier should be permitted…A 'bascule' or lifting bridge would perhaps save some small amount of time in the passage of vessels; it would render the alteration of the level of Tooley Street unnecessary, and would admit of a footway served by hydraulic lifts being practicable from shore to shore, when the bridge was open for river traffic. Further, I see no difficulty, if the latter system be adopted, in spanning the whole of the side openings between the piers on each side of the fairway and the river banks in one span. This would render the construction of side piers unnecessary, and would be a convenience to the side channels…I quite agree with you in the impossibility of making any estimate of the cost at the present moment, but no doubt an approximate estimate might be ready shortly. I may perhaps be permitted to say that any of the three designs shown in the sketches would in my judgment be an ornament to the Port of London."

Barry later explained, "It will be seen that there are two beams balanced on two upright posts, the inner ends of the beams being attached by chains to a hinged platform across the canal, and the outer ends having counter-balance weights on them. As the outer or landward ends of the beams are lowered, the inner ends are raised and pull up the hinged platform and thus open the bridge for the passage of craft…The Bridge House Estates Committee of the Corporation of London…came to the conclusion to recommend the Corporation to…promote a Bill for the erection at the Tower site of a "bascule" bridge as the best means of meeting the case. After the original sketches made by Sir Horace Jones…it was seen that any arched form of construction across the central opening would be very objectionable; as the masts of ships would be in danger of striking the arch unless they were kept exactly in the centre of the span. …we decided that any girders over the central span, when open for the passage of ships, must be horizontal and not arched."

Building the Bridge

The Corporation finally appealed to Parliament in 1885 for permission to authorize the funds to build the bridge. In doing so, it felt that it had finally reconciled the needs of the land traffic with those of the water traffic, the latter primarily as it related to ships going to and from London's famous Upper Pool business district. According to waterways expert Sir Terence Conran, this area, which is located east of the bridge, "is known as the Pool of London, which from Roman times through to the building of enclosed docks in the 19th century accounted for much of the wealth, growth and prominence of London. However, the economic prosperity generated by shipping did not stop the surrounding area from being desperately poor; it was an urban slum that haunted the novels of Charles Dickens from Oliver Twist, his first, to *Our Mutual Friend*, his last…there is Horsleydown Lane, where some say King John was thrown from his horse; the lane lay on the edge of Horsey Downe, a large field used for fairs. Then there is Shad Thames, now the best surviving example of the dramatic canyons formed by warehouses in the area: the name is a corruption of 'St John at Thames', a reference to the period when the area was settled by an Order of the Knights Templar in the 12th century. John Courage's Anchor Brewery was opened in Shad Thames in 1789…"

Given its importance, it is no surprise that the traffic around the Pool of London literally shaped the Tower Bridge, dictating "the general arrangement of the spans of the bridge," specifically with a narrow, approximately 180 feet center opening and two wider side openings, each nearly 300 feet across.

A mid-19th century depiction of the Pool of London

In spite of these plans, the watermen still opposed the bridge, insisting it would hamper their work. The men serving on the Thames Conservancy Board also complained, but their opposition fell on deaf ears as both Houses of Parliament eventually passed the bill authorizing the bridge and specifying the following:

"(1) A central opening span of 200 feet clear width, with a height of 135 feet above Trinity high water when open, and a height of 29 feet when closed against vessels with high masts. (It may be mentioned in passing that the height of the centre arch of London Bridge is 29feet above Trinity high water.

(2) The size of the piers to be 185 feet in length and 70 feet in width.

(3) The length of each of the two side spans to be 270 feet in the clear."

At the insistence of the conservators, those working on the bridge had to, at all times, maintain a swath 160 feet wide in the river through which ships and boats could pass. This meant that each of the two piers supporting the bridge had to be built separately.

In spite of these and other delays, on June 21, 1886, work finally began on the bridge. In his opening remarks, the speaker opening the ceremonies reminded his audience of the history of the organization charged with financing the endeavor, saying, "The Corporation of London has possessed for centuries estates charged with the maintenance of London Bridge. These estates were partly bestowed by generous citizens, and partly derived from gifts made at the Chapel of St. Thomas a Becket on London Bridge, for the maintenance of the bridge...the Committee charged with the management of the Bridge House Estates brought up to the Court, by the hand of their chairman, Mr. Frank Green, in 1884, a full and exhaustive report, with plans, recommending that application be made to Parliament for powers to construct a new bridge across the River Thames from the Tower; which was agreed to. In the Session of 1885, the same Committee, under the chairmanship of Mr. Thomas Beard, successfully promoted a Bill in Parliament authorizing the construction of a bridge...Its completion within the space of four years...will supply a paramount need that has been sorely felt by dwellers and workers on the north and south sides of the Thames below London Bridge, and at the same time will greatly relieve the congested traffic across that ancient and famous thoroughfare."

For its part, the *Echo* reported, "The much-discussed, long-delayed Tower Bridge is to take definite shape at last. The work will be commenced this evening by the Prince of Wales, and in due time it will be possible for the road traffic between Limehonse and Deptford, or Shadwell and Rotherhithe, to escape the long, weary round by London Bridge. The wonder is that East London has put up with the inconvenience so long...To the North of that long stretch of bridgeless river there is a population equal to that of Liverpool, Manchester, and Glasgow rolled into one. To the South there is another great and growing population that has suffered seriously for want of communication with the North side. It has never been denied that it was possible to bridge the Thames below London-bridge. In a well-governed city the step would have been taken long ago; but experience of the City Corporation and the Metropolitan Board of Works has taught the East-end to subdue its natural aspirations, and to expect nothing, so that it should not be disappointed...At last, after a more than usually prolonged talking stage, East London is to have a substitute for the Thames Subway. We congratulate the fifteen hundred thousand people on the promised possession of a bridge. We congratulate the City Corporation on being able to make up its mind. We congratulate the frequenters of London-bridge on the prospect of a relief from the congestion of traffic that great commercial highways resents; and if certain civic officials are to make a fortune out of it, that no more than others have done before them."

Oblivious to the controversy surrounding the new construction, or more likely just choosing to ignore it, Albert Edward, the Prince of Wales and future King Edward VII, marked the occasion by proclaiming, "It gives the Princess of Wales and myself sincere pleasure to be permitted on behalf of the Queen, my dear mother, to lay the first stone of the New Tower Bridge. In her name, we thank you for your loyal address, and assure you of her interest in this great undertaking. All must allow that this work, when completed, will be one of great public utility and general convenience, as tending materially to relieve the congested traffic across this noble river. We shall always retain in our remembrance this important ceremony."

Edward VII

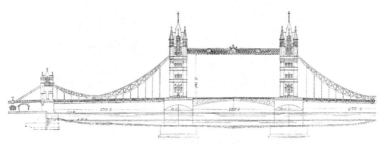

The Tower Bridge.

Length of Bridge with its approaches			2682 feet.	Depth of River at high water under central span,		33½ feet.
,, Northern approach			1000 ,,	,, ,, lowest tides ,, ,, ,,		19 ,,
,, Southern approach			800 ,,	Clear headway at high water when the leaves are		
Width between N. and S. abutments.			82o ,,	down (varies from one part of the bridge to another)		10 to 29½ feet.
,, of central span .			200 ,,	Clear headway in centre span at high water with the		
,, of side spans, each .			270 ,,	leaves raised		143 feet.

A model of the bridge

According to the *London Herald*, "As the cheers with which the conclusion of the speech of the Prince subsided, his Royal Highness advanced to the stone and placed in a cavity a bottle containing plans, coins, and newspapers of the date. The memorial stone was then lowered to its bed, and the Prince, after trying it with line and plummet, pronounced it well and truly laid…The sword and mace were then placed in saltire on the stone, and the Bishop of London read a dedicatory prayer, part of which was lost to the majority of the spectators in the booming of the guns from the adjoining battery giving forth a Royal salute. At the close of the prayer, the Chairman of the Bridge House Estates Committee, Architect, Engineer, and other gentlemen were presented to their Royal Highnesses, the first-named, Mr. Atkinson, on behalf of the Corporation, presenting the Princess with a diamond pendant in commemoration of the event…This little ceremony concluded, the National Anthem was sung by the choir of the Guildhall School of Music, and the Royal party were conducted to the entrance to the Tower by the Constable and other officers, and took their departure a midst enthusiastic cheers. Inside the Tower Gates the Coldstream Guards lined the route to the pavilion, where a guard of honour of the same regiment was stationed. The warders of the Tower were stationed inside the entrance to the pavilion."

The stone itself was inscribed,

THIS MEMORIAL STONE

WAS LAID BY

H.R.H. ALBERT EDWARD PRINCE OF WALES, K.G.,

ON BEHALF OF HER MAJESTY QUEEN VICTORIA,

ON MONDAY, THE 21ST JUNE, 1886,

IN THE 50TH YEAR OF HER MAJESTY'S LONG, HAPPY, AND PROSPEROUS REIGN.

THE RIGHT HON. JOHN STAPLES, Lord Mayor.

DAVID EVANS, ESQ RE, Alderman [and] Thos. Clarke, Esq. RE, Sheriffs

EDWARD ATKINSON, ESQ RE, Chairman of the Bridge House Estates Committee.

HORACE JONES, ESQ RE, City Architect.

JOHN WOLFE BARRY, ESQ RE, Engineer.

In order to facilitate the bridge's construction, and to mollify the watermen, the government allowed the builders to use a small portion of the famous Tower Ditch to construct the northern approach to the bridge. In return, the architect agreed to build the bridge in such a way as to coordinate with the ancient style and grace of the Tower of London.

Bob Collowan's picture of the Tower of London

The piers themselves are unique in that they contain the mechanisms necessary to open and close the bridge. On November 8, 1893, a reporter writing for the *Echo* had the opportunity to go deep into the bowels of the bridge. The reporter wrote, "The light of a match showed a faint gleam of water in the gulf below. There were nine feet of it, in fact—not from the river; that flowed in its bed far above us, for the foundations of the Tower Bridge go seventy feet below the bed of the Thames, and we were in one of the buttresses." He continued, "The water— fresh, clear, and potable—bubbled from a spring that had been struck in digging out a foothold for the huge structure whose mass of stone and iron towered hundreds of feet overhead, for the summits of the towers are 275 feet above Trinity water-mark, and we were a long way beneath the keels of the ships, and the flowing channel in which they rode…We retraced our steps along the bricked tunnel into the counterpoise pit. You do not see any bricks about the Tower Bridge from the outside; there are 31,000,000 of them nevertheless. Another thing you do not see is the mighty framework—the bones of steel and iron--for the stone casing of the towers is little more than an ornamental skin. You do see the ponderous chains interlocked in double festoons; but you do not see the anchors with which they grip the earth 45 feet underground."

After descending those 45 feet, he described the sight: "There are 350 tons of…lead for the counterpoise, and, of course, the same quantity in the pit on the other side. Looking upwards, there was a sweep of mighty cogs, and the ponderous ends of the bascule, which, with its fellow, will bridge the space of 200 feet between the towers, and when a steamer wants to pass through, will fly back against the face of the tower with as little trouble as if it were the lid of a watch, though not so rapidly."

The first step in building the piers was to construct heavy duty iron and wood caissons that could be sunk into the riverbed. One article described these in detail for readers: "The caissons used for securing the foundation of the piers consisted of strong boxes of wrought iron, without either top or bottom. To secure a good foundation it was found necessary to sink them to a depth of about 21 feet into the bed of the river. There were twelve caissons for each pier. On the north and south sides of each pier was a row of four caissons, each 28 feet square, joined at either end by a pair of triangular caissons, formed approximately to the shape of the finished pier…The caissons enclosed a rectangular space 34 feet by 124½ feet. The space was not excavated until the permanent work forming the outside portion of the pier had been built, in the caissons and between them, up to a height of 4 feet above high-water mark…First came the building of the caisson upon wooden supports over the site where it was to be sunk. The caisson was 19 feet in height and it was divided horizontally into two lengths. The lower portion was known as the permanent caisson and the upper portion, which was removable when the pier was completed, was called the temporary caisson. The object of this upper portion was simply to keep out water while the pier was being built…When ready the supports were removed and the permanent caisson lowered to the riverbed (this had previously been levelled by divers) by means of four powerful screws attached to four lowering rods. After the caisson had reached the ground various lengths of temporary caisson were added to the permanent section, till the top of the temporary portion came above the level of high water."

Unfortunately, each time time a caisson was lowered, there was a danger that something might go wrong, and eventually something did. According to J.E. Tuit, an engineer for Sir William

Arrol and Co., "The first was due to the removal of some moorings from near the site of one of the square caissons at the north pier, which had left a hole…and, after two days of tide-work, the water was excluded. Two more days had passed…when…the water rushed in through a rent in the clay, which extended to a depth of about 9in. below the cutting edge. … The temporary caisson was therefore made 2ft. higher by a couple of timbers bolted all round the top, and the sinking was continued by divers to a depth of 11 ft. below the ordinary level. … The sluices were then opened, and three days were allowed for the concrete to set before the water in the caisson was again pumped out…The second blow took place in one of the angle caissons at the south pier, and was due to a stage pile in the narrow space between the two angle caissons being driven in a slanting direction so that, as the caisson went down, its cutting edge came in contact with the pile, and thus loosened the clay in the immediate neighborhood. … The adjoining angle caisson had been previously sunk, and the blow being in the space between the two, all danger of another mishap was averted by driving the piles and removing the water from the narrow space between them, before again pumping."

Once these rooms were in place, pumps extracted the water from them and created an environment in which men could dig into the riverbed to pour the foundations for the piers. As they dug, the men continued to shore up the caissons, working to a depth of more than 50 feet below the surface of the river. In 1888, *Iron* reported, "There caissons are filled with Portland cement concrete up to the top to a certain level and from that point upwards the piers are constructed of Cornish and brickwork in Portland cement. On each each of the piers a lofty tower will be erected, the top which will receive the Upper ends of the suspension chains of the side spans, and will also support the high level foot bridge across the central opening."

In spite of these and other setbacks, progress continued until the piers actually reached the fetid air that hovered above the Thames during the Victorian Era. In order to make this moment possible, the men digging in the caissons had moved more than 30,000 cubic yards of mud and clay from the bottom of the mighty river and replaced it with even more cement, bricks and Cornish granite. A few days later, those watching the progress could clearly see the two mammoth piers that would soon support the mighty towers that would make the bridge an icon. Each one was guaranteed to hold more than 70,000 tons of steel and stone, not to mention the heavy iron works of the bridge itself. Finally, each pier, as it emerged from the riverbed itself, was faced with Cornish granite slabs, each more than two feet thick.

With the piers in place, it was time to begin construction on the towers themselves, and soon an advertisement appeared proclaiming, "Notice is hereby given that the Bridge House Estate Committee of the Corporation of London will MEET at Guildhall, on FRIDAY, the 10th day of May next, to receive TENDERS for the SUPPLY, DELIVERY, AND ERECTION OF THE IRON AND STEEL WORK OF THE SUPERSTRUCTURE OF THE TOWER BRIDGE. Drawings and specification may be seen at the office of Mr. J. Wolfe Barry, the engineer of the bridge…and copies of the drawings, specification, quantities, and form of Tender may be obtained there on loan, on deposit of one hundred pounds, which, except in the case of the contractor whose Tender is accepted, will be returned to all who tend in a bonifide Tender and return all the documents." It was signed, "JOHN A. BRAND, Comptroller of the Bridge House Estates. Guildhall, 2nd April 1889.

A few months later, in July 1889, *Lloyd's Weekly Newspaper* reported, "At a meeting of the Court of Common council, held at the Guildhall on Thursday, the Lord Mayor presiding, contracts were sealed between the corporation and Messrs. Arrol and Biggart for the construction of the iron and steel work of the superstructure of the Tower Bridge for the sum of 337,113 [pounds] and between Mr. H. H. Bartlett and the corporation for the construction of the masonry, brickwork, and carpentry of the superstructure of the same bridge for 149,122 [pounds]. In reply to questions, Mr. John Cox said the original estimate for the first-mentioned works was 250,000 [pounds…In the towers there will be hydraulic lifts for giving foot passengers access to the high-level footway, and stairs will also be provided. The mode of actucating the two leaves of the bridge will be by rotary hydraulic engines, acting through gearing on four quadrant racks applied to the rear ends of the bridge. The contract for the hydraulic machinery actuating the lifting portions of the bridge will be carried out by Sir William Armstrong, II & Co. of Elswick, who have, in conjunction Mr. Barry, worked out all the details of the machinery…The steam engines for actuating, the hydraulic machinery will be placed on the southern side of the river beneath and adjoining southern approach to the bridge. They will consist of engines of 360 horsepower each, taking steam from four boilers. Four of the accumulators will be placed upon the piers and two upon the south side of the river. The weight of steel and iron in the chain girders will be about 7,000 tons. Each of the bridge will weigh about 350 tons. The superarea of each leaf will be about 5,000 square feet."

A picture of the bridge being constructed

A Description of the Bridge

Tower Bridge in 1900

The Tower of London and Tower Bridge in the early 20th century

When completed, the bridge was covered in 235,000 cubic feet of stonework, part of it Cornish granite and the rest Portland stone. Underneath were 31 million bricks, 70,000 cubic yards of concrete, 20,000 tons of cement, and 14,000 tons of iron and steel. It was built in three parts, with suspension bridges on either side held up by heavy chains anchored to land and then draped over abutment towers. At their tallest, the chains reach more than 140 feet above the water line. In the center is a pair of high level walkways that give those with the courage to walk them an amazing view of the river and the city. The lower level of the center features a drawbridge that can open to allow tall ships to pass through.

Of course, the most spectacular part of the bridge is its pair of tall towers, each with an octagonal column at each of its four corners. Each column is more than five feet across and more than 100 feet tall and rose from atop a huge, watertight piece of granite, to which it was affixed with giant bolts holding it to the pier itself. The first landing stands 60 feet above the foundational piers and supports that bascule bridge. The second landing is 28 feet above it, and the third landing is another 28 feet up and opens onto the two upper walkways.

A modern picture of the towers

In the late 1930s, *Wonders of World Engineering* explained the special concerns caused by covering steel with stone: "It was important that precautions should be taken to prevent any adhesion between the masonry and the steelwork of the towers. With this object the columns were covered with canvas as the masonry was built round them, and spaces were left in places where any later deformation of the steelwork might bring undue weight upon the adjacent stonework. The masonry covering forms an excellent protection against extremes of temperature. All parts of the metal not accessible for painting purposes after the bridge was completed were coated thoroughly with Portland cement…Manholes were provided in the steel columns to make it possible to paint the interior whenever it became necessary. The abutments of the bridge, which were built by means of cofferdams in the usual manner and without difficulty, have similar but shorter towers."

Then there was the matter of the walkways. The article continued, "These are cantilever structures, each with a suspended span. They were built out from either tower simultaneously. The footways are cantilevers for a distance of 55 feet from either tower and suspended girders for the remaining distance of 120 feet between the cantilever ends." Furthermore, "Along the upper boom of the footway run the great ties connecting the suspension chains at their river ends. Each of the two ties is 301 feet long and is composed of eight plates 2 feet deep and 1 inch thick, ending in large eye-plates to take the pins uniting them to the suspension chains...Each chain is composed of two parts, or links, the shorter dipping from the top of the abutment tower to the roadway, the longer rising from the roadway to the summit of the main tower. The links have each a lower and upper boom, connected by diagonal bracing so as to form a rigid girder. They were built in the positions they had to occupy, supported on trestles, and were not freed until they had been joined by huge steel pins to the ties crossing the central span and to those on the abutment towers."

For all its beauty, the bridge could never have been built had it not been able to open and close to allow river traffic to pass through. Each of the two leaves that could open to an 86 degree angle is about 160 feet long and weigh more than 1,000 tons. In 1907, one reporter noted, "Few enterprises have more completely justified their existence than the Tower Bridge. The bascules open and shut so easily, that the hydraulic lifts for passengers, says the 'Daily News,' are hardly used at all, for every one prefers to watch the ships go by and wait until the roadway swings into its place again. So absorbing has this amusement apparently become, that the Monument has gone quite melancholy over the falling-off in its receipts...The country cousins who were generally good for at lease some £120 a month, now despise clambering up its stone steps to pay three pence for a grimy view, when they can go up to the Tower Bridge for nothing, and have a far finer sight from the high level footway. So true is it, that when your British public can get a thing for nothing in one place, it will not pay a cent in another for a similar enjoyment."

C.M. Lee's picture of a tall ship going through the bridge

The process was, and is, something to see. For one thing, there was the matter of where the power to move the giant leaves would come from. On the south side of the river near the bridge was a simple looking building that served a mighty purpose, for inside it were housed two large pools holding the water that would be called into use to open and close the bridge. When pressed into service, the water shot out of its tank under 700 to 800 pounds of pressure per square inch.

Since the ability to move ships past the bridge was critical, as was the ability to lower the bridge and restore street traffic, Tower Bridge had not one but two engines, one on each side of the river. Both could do the jobs necessary to keep the bridge operational, so there was always a backup. Likewise, the bridgehouse was always guarded against unwelcome intruders who might tamper with its mechanisms, which is understandably of great comfort to anyone who has ever crossed a drawbridge and had a fleeting fear it might open under their feet. Fortunately, there was more than one method of prevention for this; for example, when the bridge was down, the leaves locked together with bolts powered by hydraulic energy, ensuring that even if something went wrong with the mechanics controlling the bridge, they would still lock gently together.

One of the original steam engines

Of course, what was perhaps most amazing was the speed with which the bridge could be raised and lowered. From the moment the first gear began to turn to raise the bridge, through the time it took for a ship to pass, to the time that the bridge was lowered and normal traffic patterns were restored, less than five minutes would pass. Likewise, the lifts, each of which could carry up to 18 passengers to the walkway more than 10 stories above, took less than one minute. One can almost imagine Victorian gentlemen in top hats pulling out their pocket watches to time how long it took the bridge to open and close on any given occasion and nodding in approval each time the bridge master shaved a few seconds off his previous time.

Opening the Bridge

The big day finally came on July 2, 1894. That afternoon, all sorts of pageantry commemorated the official opening of the Tower Bridge. One paper described the affair: "Many and splendid as have been the pageants witnessed in the City of London during its long Municipal life, few have been more brilliant, or will have a more abiding and historic interest, than that of Saturday last, when the Prince of Wales, on behalf of the Queen, opened the great Tower Bridge, which is one of the latest undertakings that the people of the Metropolis owe to the public spirit of the Cooperation. The occasion was one which drew together all classes in a common fellowship…It gratified the popular desire for spectacular display; it emphasized once more the value of the services rendered by the ancient Corporation to the commerce and industry of London; and it furnished the opportunity for such an expression of loyalty towards the Royal family as has not often been surpassed in the City annals. The day was ideally perfect in the all-important matter of the weather, the arrangements were admirably conceived and carried out, and the Royal procession from Marlborough House to the Bridge, and the return by water, was one long ovation of the most gratifying and enthusiastic kind."

In his speech, the Prince of Wales declared, "It is a great satisfaction to the Princess of Wales and myself to be permitted on behalf of the Queen, my dear mother, to open the Tower Bridge across the River Thames, and we thank you for your loyal and dutiful address on the occasion. This Bridge will be an enduring monument of the well-directed energy and public spirit of the Corporation of London; it will also serve as an example of the splendid engineering skill bestowed on its construction…Linking two busy and populous districts of the Metropolis, the Bridge will afford immediately increased facilities of communication, and be of the greatest service to the industrious inhabitants of these districts; while from its ingenious and admirable arrangement it will not interfere with the navigation of the river."

The plague commemorating the auspicious day read simply, "This Bridge was opened by HRH the Prince of Wales, KG on behalf of Her Majesty Queen Victoria, on Saturday the 30th June 1894 in the presence of HRH The Princess of Wales, HRH The Duke of York KG and other members of the Royal Family, the Right Honorable Sir George Robert Tyler, Bart., Lord Mayor." Below this inscription were 43 names, including "2 Sheriffs, 1 Engineer, 8 Members of the Bridge House Estates Committee, 31 Commoners and 1 Comptroller of the Bridge House Estates."

Despite the great fanfare, not everyone was thrilled with the bridge. On July 31, the wire services reported, "Thomas Cantwell and Charles Quinn, two anarchists charged with inciting persons, to murder members of the royal family on the day preceding the opening of the Tower bridge, are on trial at the Old Bailey. The prisoners, it appears, the day before the opening of the Tower bridge, succeeded in getting together a crowd about them on Tower Hill."

The article went on to relate how Cantwell mounted the parapet of a wall and displayed a placard that read, "Tower Bridge Fellow Workers:—You have expended life, energy and skill in building this bridge. Now come the royal vermin and, the rascally politicians, with pomp and splendor, to claim all the credit. You are condemned to the workhouse and paupers' graves to glorify these lazy swine who live upon our labor. I heard men saying 'leave tears and praying. The sharp knife heedeth not the sheep.' Are we not stronger than the rich?'"

Unfortunately, anarchists were not the only ones who marred the joyous atmosphere brought about by the new bridge. Less than two months after it opened, the *Westminster Budget* ran an article aptly titled, "A STUDY IN SUICIDE". It began, "It is difficult to understand why the

Tower Bridge should have so rapidly come into favour that it already rivals Waterloo Bridge as a popular suicide resort. But it certainly has done so, for already, during the brief time which has elapsed since its opening, five men have dropped from its heights into the river below."

The author then quoted a policeman stationed on the bridge, who opined, "I cannot see why men who want to commit suicide should select this bridge to do it from. The only thing that suggests itself to me is the novelty of the idea—and that will not last long at this rate. There may be one other point. People read that another man has 'jumped off the Tower Bridge' and they at once run away with the idea that the attempted suicide took place from off the high footway...That is nonsense—nobody can get off that footway. It is from the lower level bridge that the men have jumped— though even that is high enough—and they have been lucky in not hurting themselves in the fall, although they were prevented from drowning. But if it were possible for a man to go off the high bridge, he would be almost sure to break half the bones in his body in the fall."

In answer to the question, "Is there anything about this bridge, then, to tempt a man to suicide?" the bobby responded, "No, of course not. But if a man were looking for a chance to commit suicide, I could quite understand his preferring this bridge to any other. In my opinion a great many of the attempts at suicide are made on the impulse of the moment. You know that a man standing on a great height often has a giddy feeling, and has to hold himself back almost to prevent himself from jumping over. Well, I think it is something like that here...A man leans over the parapet, as he is crossing the bridge, to watch the water rushing through underneath. The parapet is low, and instead of being an enormous wall of stone, it is just a nicely-polished wooden rail. He feels some sudden impulse and over he goes. Of course there are 'drunks' and men who are sick of starving—I can understand why they go over. But I think my idea is right in many cases."

The article finally concluded, "Whatever may be the incentive to jump over, the act is being guarded against with great care. There were quite half-a-dozen policemen posted on the bridge while our informant was explaining his view of the situation, and they appeared to have nothing at all to do, so they may have been told off simply to interfere with intending suicides."

Once the bridge was completed, it had to be maintained. In 1910, less than 15 years after it opened for business, some repairs had to be made. According to one reporter at the time, "Naturally a great deal of money has to be paid out each year for repairs, and some idea of this may be given by referring to the cost of repainting Tower bridge about a couple of years ago. One hundred men were engaged on the work night and day and to give three coats of paint to every inch of the ironwork required about sixty tons of paint. Miles of scaffolding were erected to make the work safe: but, at the same time, the men employed were covered by special insurance...Besides the illumination given by carbide lamps of 2500 candlepower, hundreds of pounds of candles were used nightly by the workmen. Gilding the large crestings of the bridge, and the city arms and shields on the footways cost $2000, while the total cost was about $30,000. The interval allowed between each painting of the bridge is six years, so that for this work alone the expenditure on Tower bridge is $5,000 a year."

The turn of the 20th century brought with it all kinds of new technology, especially in the world of travel. Airplanes were seen more and more often in the skies above London and other large cities as pilots tried one new trick after another, and inevitably, the Tower Bridge became a prop for one man's exploits. On August 12, 1912, the *London Standard* told readers about one such stunt: "A British airman, Mr. F. K. McClean, on a British hydro-aeroplane (a Short) has gained the honour of being the first aviator to fly up the Thames to Westminster and to alight on the river after skimming the water and passing under the arches of several of the bridges. ... Mr. McClean arrived shortly before 8 o'clock, and was first seen like a speck between but away beyond the towers of Tower Bridge. At first many of the spectators refused to believe that the object was an aeroplane."

For his part, McClean recalled, "I just thought I'd come. I had an engagement in London at midday, and I've done the journey from Eastchurch, 68 miles, in 80 minutes. ... At first I was not sure what to do in the case of the Tower Bridge, but when I get to it I went between the roadway and the upper footway. You see, the arches of the bridges are big things when you get near to them."

For all that the Tower Bridge today represents London to people around the world, it has not always been popular. At the time of its completion in 1894, *The Builder* complained that the towers gave "the appearance of carrying immense suspension chains which they could not possibly carry. The writer added, "Although the masonry towers are only envelopes and could not possibly carry the chains which appear to be suspended across them, they have as least the aspect of being solidly built towers founded on the piers which carry the bridge. But even this is a delusion. Will it be credited that these masonry towers are actually built on and carried by the ironwork; their side walls have no foundations at all—they are slung, as it were in gigantic stirrups of steel, and at the period of our visit to the works you could actually look under the base of the walls into a vacant space above which they were banging...What will be the ultimate result of the masonry of this depending on a large steel structure which must be subject to constant movement future years will have to show. What strikes one at present is that the whole structure is the most monstrous and preposterous architectural sham that we have ever known of, and is in that sense a discredit to the generation which has erected it...Far better would it have been to have built simply the naked steal work, and let the construction show us what it really is: the effect, if somewhat bare looking, would have been at least honest and we should have been relieved from the spectacle of many thousands spent on what is not the bridge at all—what is no part of its structure—but an elaborate and costly make-believe."

Likewise, in 1916, architect H. H. Stratham complained, "The Tower Bridge...represents the vice of tawdriness and pretentiousness, and of falsification of the actual facts of the structure. It is stated that the exterior clothing was designed by an architect; he cannot have been a very eminent one, as we never hear his name; it looks to me more like what results from the advertisement we sometimes see –'Wanted immediately a draughtsman; must be an expert Gothic hand'- - it is draughtsman's architecture…The exceedingly heavy suspension chains are made to appear to hang on an ornamental stone structure which they would in reality drag down, and the side walls of the apparently solid tower rest on part of the iron structure, and you could see under them before the roadway was made up. All architects would have much preferred the plain steel structure to this kind of elaborate sham. The same kind of spirit is showing itself in the treatment of ironwork; capitals inserted where they have nothing to do with the structure, spandrils filled in with bad Gothic tracery, and so on. If iron is designed on good lines, it will look better in itself without these gewgaws."

Stratham later softened his remarks, saying, "Sir Horace Jones's design would have been better for greater simplicity, and especially for the omission of the unnecessary and trivial projecting bay windows or oriels at the sides in the lower portion. But in the main it is a fine and massive design, with a good deal of character about it, and it had the merit of being really what it pretended to be—a solid masonry tower." Nonetheless, he couldn't help but take more shots at the bridge: "When the engineer came to the unfortunate decision to make the towers a sham skin of masonry hiding a real construction of steel, after Sir Horace Jones's death, the design was put into the hands of another architect… He may have received orders merely to modify Sir Horace Jones's design; and people who know nothing of architectural detail may think it only amounts to that…But every architect can see that the result is that, while one or two weak points in Sir Horace Jones's design have been retained, every good quality it had has been re moved and the whole thing hopelessly vulgarised. It is therefore absurd, and a gross injustice to Sir Horace Jones, to speak of the towers as they now stand as his design. As I said before, they are specimens of draughtsman's architecture."

Stratham also quoted J. E. Tuit, who had served as an engineer for the contractors, as saying, "On comparing it with the structure which has now been completed, it will be seen that so many modifications have been made that practically only the principle of Mr. Jones's early design has been retained." Stratham insisted, however, that, "In a structural sense, even the principle has not been retained; but the remark forms a strong independent testimony to the truth of my statement that the towers as now erected cannot be regarded as Sir Horace Jones's design, and that it is absurd to call them so."

Due to its fame and prominence, Tower Bridge often finds itself at the center of some sort of protest, the most dangerous and dramatic of which occurred in 1968. On April 5 of that year, the *Associated Press* reported, "A jet fighter plane buzzed the House of Commons twice at noon Friday and then flew under the upper part of Tower Bridge, skimming only feet above the busy traffic. … The pilot flew between the two towers and between the roadway and footway." It was later determined that the pilot, Alan Pollock, pulled the stunt to protest the lack of aerial displays at the RAF's 50 year anniversary celebration. He later admitted that he never set out to fly through the bridge: "Until this very instant I'd had absolutely no idea that, of course, Tower Bridge would be there. It was easy enough to fly over it, but the idea of flying through the spans suddenly struck me. I had just ten seconds to grapple with the seductive proposition which few ground attack pilots of any nationality could have resisted. My brain started racing to reach a decision. Years of fast low-level strike flying made the decision simple..."

A 1950s picture of a Royal Air Force plane in the river with the Tower Bridge behind it

In the years following World War II, many of the warehouses near the river closed, making Tower Bridge less necessary, so in an effort to shore up its commercial appeal, the Corporation began a long, arduous process to rebrand the bridge as a tourist destination. In 1975, the Board replaced the steam engines with electric motors, modernizing the way in which both the drawbridge and the lifts operated. It also began to explore the possibility of reopening the walkways.

Initially, many opposed their efforts, claiming that the walkways were a nuisance that attracted those contemplating suicide, but when one considers the number of people who use the bridge each year, there have been a surprisingly small number of suicides. Ultimately, this problem was solved by enclosing the formerly open walkways in glass in 1982. The *Associated Press* reported, "Tower Bridge, the sturdy landmark over the Thames, has reopened for the first time in 7 years in a celebration of Victorian durability and eccentricity. ... Now the walkways and the floor below in both towers are thronged by tourists who come for the view, and to see exhibits about the bridge's history, including its still operational original lifting mechanism. ...2,000 to 3,000 people a day are visiting the reopened towers."

John Fielding, then the tourist manager for the bridge, added, "It's London's Eiffel Tower. There's nothing quite like it in the world. Certainly there are bigger and more splendid bridges, but this is unique, the most instantly recognizable." Concerning why it had ever been closed, explained, "Pedestrians soon found it was too much effort to climb up those stairs when the drawbridge was open, especially since the bridge mechanism can open and close in under six minutes. The walkways became a haven for derelicts, so they were closed to the public and only reopened with the renovation completed last June 30."

The interior of the walkway

One of the most amazing events in the bridge's history took place in the post-war years. According to writer David Ellis, "AS EVENING began falling across London on December 30, 1952, bus driver Albert Gunter must have wondered if he'd lapsed into a nightmare as he started driving his Number 78 bus across Tower Bridge straddling the River Thames. For the centre of the bridge comprises two 30m-long hinged bascules (or leaves) that open upwards at over 80 degrees to allow ships to pass through. To his horror, the one he was on was rising at an increasingly sickening angle right under his bus and its 20 passengers...Making a split-second decision, Albert dropped two gears and gunned the engine of the cumbersome double-decker as fast as it would go - miraculously leaping the vehicle forward from the bascule, and somehow 'flying' it through mid-air to drop, deafeningly but still upright, almost two metres down on to the opposite leaf that had not yet begun to rise. His conductor suffered a broken leg, 12 passengers received minor injuries, and Albert himself was given a 10-pound reward for his heroics...with a subsequent inquiry finding the bascule had been raised due to a mix-up between staff."

In April 2011, *The Evening Standard* of London reported on the status of the bridge ahead of the approaching 2012 Summer Olympics:

> "TOWER Bridge, one of London's most prominent landmarks, is to undergo a lighting makeover. An energy-efficient system will be installed before the Olympics to help reduce energy bills and cut carbon emissions. It will also enhance the world-famous structure's architectural features at night. Tower Bridge's gothic turrets, central aerial walkway and suspension chains will be bathed in colours sensitive to its listed building status.

> "The lighting system...will be flexible so the intensity of light, as well as the colours, can be varied. This means, for example, that it could be spectacularly lit up in the colours of the Union Jack during the 2012 Games. The bridge currently has traditional, static floodlighting which can flatten the architecture and has not been upgraded for 25 years. The makeover, which follows major repainting work, will be funded at no cost to the taxpayer by energy firms EDF and GE and the bridge's owner, the City of London Corporation."

Along with the rest of the nation, Boris Johnson, who arranged the transformation, insisted, "I want London to look its very best in 2012 as the eyes of the world are upon us. Tower Bridge is one of this city's most stunning landmarks, recognized the world over and therefore deserving of a star role in these year-long celebrations. I am thrilled to have brokered this deal to bathe Tower Bridge in ecofriendly light to create a fresh perspective of this wonderful icon. This is another great legacy for London stretching for decades beyond the Olympic year."

A picture of Tower Bridge during the 2012 Olympics

By this time, many Londoners had become completely dependent on the bridge to complete their morning commutes. That is why there was such an outcry when word came it would have to be closed for repairs. *The Evening Standard* told readers, "TOWER BRIDGE will be shut to traffic for three months from October 1 amid warnings of gridlock on both sides of the Thames. The Victorian landmark will be closed to vehicles and bicycles while it undergoes maintenance. Black cab drivers calculate that even the shortest river crossing could take up to 30 minutes longer at peak times. Works being undertaken include replacing the decking on the bridge's bascules plus removing rust, mechanical repairs and road resurfacing…More than 40,000 motorists and pedestrians cross Tower Bridge every day. Pedestrians will also be banned from the bridge for three weekends during the works, with the possibility of a free ferry to move them across the river. Cabbies today questioned the timing of the works. But the City of London Corporation said this was because it is when the Thames is quietest for riverboat traffic." In spite of the outcry, Chris Hayward, the head of London's planning and transport committee, insisted: "This decision to close Tower Bridge has not been taken lightly. We will use this time to repair, refurbish, and upgrade London's most iconic bridge, which has gone without significant engineering works for more than 35 years."

In 1993, as the bridge approached its 100 year anniversary, those in charge created a special exhibition chronicling the first century of the bridge's history. There were videos showing grainy black and white photographs of the bridge as it rose up above the Thames, as well as animatronic workmen explaining their hardships in building the marvel. There were also exhibit cases full of machinery, as well as large panels giving details about the logistics behind constructing the bridge.

Today, according to the Tower's website, the exhibition continues: "Tower Bridge Exhibition is the most exciting way to explore the most famous bridge in the world. From the modern high-level Walkways and its spectacular new glass floor to the historic Engine Rooms and towers; Tower Bridge Exhibition tells the history of the bridge explaining how and why it came into existence. By way of our grand Victorian staircase or fully accessible lift, visitors are invited to travel back in time to the nineteenth century. From the North tower, explore the fascinating history of Tower Bridge: its significance and its function; its place in history and in the heart of the nation…A short bespoke video shown by artist, Stephen Biesty, depicting the construction of the Bridge can be enjoyed in the South Tower before wandering down the beautiful staircase, complemented by 'Battersea to Bermondsey', LED-lit motion sensitive artworks showing iconic buildings along the Thames. The experience culminates in a visit to the Victorian Engine Rooms, which houses one of London's true hidden gems: huge and beautifully maintained steam engines, furnaces and accumulators that were once used to power the raising of Tower Bridge's 'bascules' – the moveable roadways at the bridge's centre. Exciting hands-on mechanisms and information panels will explain the ingenious hydraulic technology used over the years to keep the bridge in motion."

For those with a more adventurous spirit, the website informs readers, "Moving through to the high-level Walkways, visitors will be able to experience our biggest and most exciting development to the Exhibition since it originally opened: the Glass Floor – a unique viewpoint of London life. Make sure to plan your visit for the chance to see the magic of the bridge lifting beneath your feet!" At the same time, visitors who prefer not to look down can still "admire stunning panoramic views from the Walkways, spying popular London landmarks such as St Paul's Cathedral and the Monument to the west and St Katharine Docks leading to Canary Wharf to the east."

Online Resources

Other books about English history by Charles River Editors

Further Reading

Westminster Abbey

Bradley, S. and N. Pevsner (2003) The Buildings of England – London 6: Westminster, New Haven: Yale University Press, pp. 105–207.

Mortimer, Richard ed., Edward the Confessor: The Man and the Legend, The Boydell Press, 2009. Eric Fernie, 'Edward the Confessor's Westminster Abbey', pp. 139–150. Warwick Rodwell, 'New Glimpses of Edward the Confessor's Abbey at Westminster', pp. 151–167. Richard Gem, Craftsmen and Administrators in the Building of the Confessor's Abbey', pp. 168–172.

Harvey, B. (1993) Living and Dying in England 1100–1540: The Monastic Experience, Ford Lecture series, Oxford: Clarendon Press.

Morton, H. V. [1951] (1988) In Search of London, London: Methuen.

Trowles, T. (2008) Treasures of Westminster Abbey, London: Scala.

Tower of London

Allen Brown, Reginald; Curnow, P (1984), Tower of London, Greater London: Department of the Environment Official Handbook, Her Majesty's Stationery Office

Blunt, Wilfred (1976), The Ark in the Park: The Zoo in the Nineteenth Century, Hamish Hamilton, ISBN 0-241-89331-3

Cathcart King, David James (1988), The Castle in England and Wales: an Interpretative History, Croom Helm

Creighton, Oliver (2002), Castles and Landscapes, Continuum

Impey, Edward; Parnell, Geoffrey (2000), The Tower of London: The Official Illustrated History, Merrell Publishers in association with Historic Royal Palaces

Jerome, Fiona (2006), Tales from the Tower: Secrets and Stories from a Gory and Glorious Past, Think Publishing

Lapper, Ivan; Parnell, Geoffrey (2000), The Tower of London: A 2000-year History, Osprey Publishing

Liddiard, Robert (2005), Castles in Context: Power, Symbolism and Landscape, 1066 to 1500, Windgather Press Ltd

Parnell, Geoffrey (1993), The Tower of London, Batsford

Sellers, Leonard (1997), Shot in the Tower: The Story of the Spies executed in the Tower of London during the First World War, Leo Cooper

Strickland, Agnes (1840), Lives of the Queens of England from the Norman Conquest. Volume II, Henry Colburn

Wilson, Derek (1998) [1978], The Tower of London: A Thousand Years (2nd ed.), Allison & Busby

Buckingham Palace

Goring, O. G. (1937). *From Goring House to Buckingham Palace*. London: Ivor Nicholson & Watson.

Harris, John; de Bellaigue, Geoffrey; & Miller, Oliver (1968). *Buckingham Palace*. London: Nelson.

Healey, Edma (1997). *The Queen's House: A Social History of Buckingham Palace*. London: Penguin Group.

Mackenzie, Compton (1953). *The Queen's House*. London: Hutchinson.

Nash, Roy (1980). *Buckingham Palace: The Place and the People*. London: Macdonald Futura.

Peacocke, M. D. (1951). *The Story of Buckingham Palace*. London: Odhams Press.

Robinson, John Martin (1999). *Buckingham Palace*. Published by The Royal Collection, St James's Palace, London

Wright, Patricia (1999). *The Strange History of Buckingham Palace*. Stroud, Gloucs.: Sutton Publishing Ltd.

Tower Bridge

Barry, John Wolfe. (1894) *The Tower Bridge: A Lecture.*

Billington, David P. (1985) *The Tower and the Bridge: The New Art of Structural Engineering.*

Speaker-Yuan, Margaret. (2004) *The London Tower Bridge.*

Tuit, James Edward. (1894) *The Tower Bridge: Its History and Construction from the Date of the....*

Welch, Charles. (1894) *History of the Tower Bridge and of Other Bridges Over the Thames*

Free Books by Charles River Editors

We have brand new titles available for free most days of the week. To see which of our titles are currently free, click on this link.

Discounted Books by Charles River Editors

We have titles at a discount price of just 99 cents everyday. To see which of our titles are currently 99 cents, click on this link.